SWORD, LANCE & BAYONET

T0381642

PLATE I

HENRY HERBERT, TENTH EARL OF PEMBROKE (1734–1794)
Colonel of the First Dragoons
From the portrait at Wilton House by Sir Joshua Reynolds

SWORD, LANCE & BAYONET

A Record of the Arms of the British Army & Navy

BY

CHARLES FFOULKES, C.B., O.B.E.

Hon.D.Litt., Oxon., F.S.A.

AND

CAPTAIN E. C. HOPKINSON, M.C.

" Cedit Ensis Calamo"

CAMBRIDGE

AT THE UNIVERSITY PRESS

1938

CAMBRIDGE UNIVERSITY PRESS
Cambridge, New York, Melbourne, Madrid, Cape Town,
Singapore, São Paulo, Delhi, Mexico City

Cambridge University Press
The Edinburgh Building, Cambridge CB2 8RU, UK

Published in the United States of America by Cambridge University Press, New York

www.cambridge.org
Information on this title: www.cambridge.org/9781107670150

© Cambridge University Press 1938

First published 1938
First paperback edition 2013

A catalogue record for this publication is available from the British Library

ISBN 978-1-107-67015-0 Paperback

Contents

Preface

Prior to the existence of a standing army in this country the weapons in use were those of personal idiosyncrasy, and indeed, in the early days of the organized Army, there was little control of pattern or design. The arms of the earlier periods have been studied in detail and their history can be found in the pages of any standard work on arms and armour. It has been no light task to trace and record, within the compass of one volume, the story of the gradual superannuation of these descendants of primitive weapons. Those who knew the *arme blanche* as a sight of everyday familiarity neglected to remember that the pen is mightier than the sword, and none of the students of military equipment made any serious attempt to help future generations with written or pictorial record. It would therefore seem to be left to us to recite, as well as may be, its funeral oration. Sins of omission and commission we have doubtless committed. Such as these may be, we pray the reader to forgive and ask him to remember the need for brevity and the endless and often futile research entailed.

Without generous help and advice from many the task would have been wellnigh insurmountable, and the production of this work as it stands is in no small measure due to the assistance rendered to us by the officers of the Royal Library, Windsor Castle, of the War Office Library, of the Public Record Office, of the Royal United Services Institution, by Mr J. W. Latham of the Wilkinson Sword Company and the Rev. Percy Sumner, F.S.A. We would also express our indebtedness to the Under-Secretary of State for War, the Comptroller of H.M. Stationery Office, the Officer Commanding the 15/19th Hussars, and to the Council of the Society for Army Historical Research for leave to reproduce certain illustrations and for the loan of half-tone blocks.

C. FF.
E. C. H.

London 1938

ILLUSTRATIONS

PLATES

TEXT-FIGURES

* Figures marked with an asterisk are reproduced from textbooks on small arms and prints by permission of the War Office.

NOTE. The dates given are the earliest and latest of pictorial or other records.

ILLUSTRATIONS

ILLUSTRATIONS

1. Head, 1816	7. Head, 1860
2. Shoe, 1816	8. Shoe, 1860
3. Head, 1820	9. Head, 1868
4. Point protector, 1820	10. Shoe, 1868
5. Head, 1840	11. Experimental head, ? 1895
6. Head, 1846	12. Handguard

A. Martini-Henry, 1871
B. Martini-Enfield, 1883
C. Lancaster, 1855
D. Artillery, Mark III, ? 1870
E. Pattern, 1888
F. Lee-Metford, 1907

Introduction

Man has always been and always will be a combative animal. From his excursions in search of food, to acquire territory, to safeguard his family, to avenge real or imaginary wrongs, we can trace an important part of the history of the world, illustrated by the weapons he has used.

Hands and teeth, wood, stone, bronze and iron have been in turn used and adapted by man to achieve his purpose, which was ever to obtain sovereignty and superiority over his neighbour.

We do not propose to deal with the sling and the bow in these pages, although these may be said to have been to some extent the precursors of the firearm; nor shall we discuss the evolution of the club or mace, although this weapon in its most primitive form was used by all combatants in the trench warfare on the Western Front in 1914–18. It should, however, be noted that it is from the sharpened Stone-Age club that, in the process of experiments spread over thousands of years, the sword was developed. Of all these primitive weapons the lance has remained the same tree sapling of antiquity with but a metal point added, and eventually the point taken off and attached to the firearm to form the bayonet.

Under present consideration the sword is the most important of all these weapons, and yet for centuries the most highly skilled craftsmen failed to produce a completely satisfactory weapon. The Greek, the Roman, and before him the Bronze-Age warrior realized that the true function of the sword was to attack the enemy hand to hand, the defence being achieved by the shield on the left arm. Therefore, he favoured a short well-balanced handy weapon which vanished with the Saxons and Danes only to reappear in the ornamental swords of the French Infantry of the first half of the nineteenth century, and of the British bandsmen of the Victorian period. The great swords of the mounted knight from the tenth to the fifteenth century are lacking in every quality which a sword should possess. The grips are small, the blades heavy and ill balanced and the points of little or no use for the thrust. The handguards are negligible, but that may be accounted for by the fact that the hand was protected by mail or plate. The battle-axe or mace would have been a more serviceable weapon, but these were not so favoured as the sword, which in the course of centuries became the symbol of chivalry, justice and military power.

This neglect of the essentials in defensive and offensive arms is very noticeable all through the ages. We find armour attached with straps that could easily be cut off, helmets which were often more of a hindrance than a defence, and weapons like the halberd and gisarme of such intricate design that they hampered foot soldiers in close formation, as the Swiss found after the Battle of Arebo in 1442, when they reverted to the primitive pike. In more modern times the head-dresses of Cavalry and Infantry were so entirely unsuited for campaigning that it seems incredible that they should have been designed by soldiers for soldiers; and when, to this ornate panoply is added a useless appendage like the sabretache the brain reels with this sartorial Pelion on Ossa. In the last half of the sixteenth century, when defensive armour was being gradually discarded, the long rapier with its complex handguard was developed, and at a later date the more complete guard of the broadsword found favour and eventually became identified with Cromwell's trooper and later with the Highlander. The fact that "Highland swords" were ordered for the English Cavalry in 1707 would seem to suggest that it was found to be a serviceable weapon and as such was used by Cavalry and by the Grenadiers of the Line Regiments up to 1751 if not later. We shall refer at length later on to the Lance, Halberd, Pike and other weapons, but for the present we will confine our investigations to the written or printed records which deal more particularly with the swords of the army at various periods.

Early Regulations, Warrants, and Records

EARLY REGULATIONS, WARRANTS, AND RECORDS[1]

It would be perhaps an irreverent exaggeration to say that the Army of the eighteenth century was in a state of anarchy as regards equipment, but it is an incontrovertible fact that till the beginning of the nineteenth century there were few regulations which applied to the whole Army, and these seem to have been honoured as much in the breach as in the observance. To the student of military subjects it is heart-breaking to wade through the vast mass of documents in the Public Record Office classed under the heading "W.O." which teem with warrants, out-letters, commissions, reports, pensions, ordnance records and other naval and military matters. It is true that some attempt was recently made to compile a printed index, but this serves only to raise false hopes, and the searcher finds, especially as regards arms and equipment, that the reference is to a bare fact with no details.

Take for example the Board of a round dozen of General Officers who issued an order dated 31 May 1788[2] dealing with swords for the Heavy Dragoons and Light Dragoons. This gives useful information as to the blades, which measured for the Heavy Dragoons $39 \times 1\frac{5}{12}$ in. and for the Light Dragoons $36 \times 1\frac{1}{2}$ in., the blade being curved "$1\frac{3}{4}$ inches from the straight". In the case of the former the hilts were to be "half-basket as carried by the Inniskilling Dragoons" and in the case of the latter "as now used". It has, however, been impossible to trace a previous order for these patterns and we can only assume that the Colonels of these regiments had adopted them in earlier years and that the War Department accepted them eventually as the designs for general use.

[1] Where not otherwise stated all references are to the Public Record Office.

[2] W.O. 3/27, p. 36.

(3)

The Colonel was for long supreme in the question of equipping his men, and we find that tastes differed as to whether steel or brass hilts were preferable. Indeed, some commanding officers seem to have been careless as to the actual supply of weapons to their men, and this perhaps can hardly be wondered at when it is remembered that as a rule the Colonel had to foot the bill. It was not only the Colonel who was in fault, for in some cases, after a deficiency had been reported, the Inspecting Officer passed the swords as correct. The following returns go far to show the parlous state of the Army as regards equipment in the middle of the eighteenth century, at a time when this country was conducting military operations in Europe, India and America. On 27 April 1753 the 13th Foot are reported as having "arms very bad and absolutely unfit", and on 10 September of the same year, for 700 rank and file they had only 103 swords, mostly unfit for service. On 3 November of the same year the swords of the Royal Regiment of Dragoons were scheduled "very clean but old and worn, almost all unfit for service". These had had hard service as they had been issued in 1744. The Inspecting Officer, John Campbell (Duke of Argyll), writes: "a very fine regiment and when supplied with arms will be fit for service." The King's Own Dragoons were worse off on 13 May 1754, for they reported their arms as "so worn as to be really unfit for any service". The same conditions are noted for the 3rd Foot in October of 1755 and yet John Campbell reports: "a very good regiment, well appointed."[1] Another entry under the date 1768 gives the number of sergeants of the 49th Foot as fifteen and reports all their seventeen halberds and swords as bad, the Inspecting Officer compromising by merely stating: "Arms clean." And so this goes on all through the Returns of this period with an occasional ray of hope for the Army as instanced by the report of the 12th Foot: "swords remarkably good."[2]

Evidently this question of deficiencies came to a head in

[1] W.O. 27/3.   [2] W.O. 27/14.

1768, for a Royal Warrant was issued on 19 December laying down that all sergeants and the whole of the Grenadier companies were to have swords. The Highland Regiments, however, had their own ideas on the subject, and in 1775 the Grenadiers of the 42nd Foot paraded without swords, which they considered to be "encumbrances",[1] and by 1783 they had returned all their swords to the Ordnance at Halifax, the Inspecting Officer merely noting the fact without criticism of this direct defiance of orders.

Whether other regiments followed suit or not it is impossible to say, but evidently the 42nd won the day, and an order was issued on 21 July 1784 discontinuing the use of swords for Grenadier Companies.[2] But in spite of regulations and warrants the Colonels had still some voice in the matter, for the Board of 31 May 1788 before referred to would not commit themselves as to whether British or German swords were the better, but played for safety and allowed the Colonels to have which they liked.[3] It should be remembered that means of communication were difficult and that it took a long time for an order to reach troops in Scotland, Ireland or America; and conversely, if an order were ignored it took some time for a record of the delinquency to reach the Horse Guards, and by that time the Government might have changed and with it the ruling military powers at headquarters. With the advent of the Peninsular and Waterloo campaigns, as has been the case in all wars, the important need of the moment was to carry on with the equipment available, for there was no Ministry of Munitions to organize civilian factories, and indeed, to an appreciable extent, there were few factories in this country for the production of war material, much of which came direct from Germany. If this had been otherwise Wellington might have given favourable consideration to the epoch-making invention of the Rev. Alexander Forsyth, who produced his percussion lock in 1805 and had to

[1] W.O. 27/1–60 sub anno. [2] W.O. 3/26, p. 155.
[3] W.O. 3/27, p. 37.

(5)

wait till 1839 to see its adoption by the Rifle Brigade. With the British Infantry armed with a percussion musket Wellington might not have said of Waterloo that it was "a damned serious thing...the nearest run thing in my life".[1]

When the war was over and the military authorities had time to take stock of the general confusion of orders, warrants and regulations, the Horse Guards issued the first complete *Dress Regulations* in 1822 and these have been revised from time to time up to the year 1934. In 1856 there is a tantalizing record of an order that the *Dress Regulations* were to be accompanied by coloured illustrations by a competent artist at an estimated cost of £200.[2] Either the artist could not be found, or, as is more probable, the Treasury, smarting under the cost of the Crimean War, considered, very properly, that the expenditure of so much public money was entirely unjustifiable. However, the matter was not dropped and was revived in 1866 when four volumes of *Army Equipment* were issued with the intention of illustrating the text with coloured and monochrome plates. For some unknown reason illustrations of General Officers, Cavalry and Artillery equipment were omitted. The volumes dealing with Royal Engineers, Infantry, and the Army Hospital Corps were treated in minute detail: uniform, small arms, and even axes, saws and other minutiae, being carefully illustrated. But this was too good to last and plain and unadorned *Dress Regulations* were issued periodically as occasion demanded till the advent of process reproduction led the authorities to bring out in 1900 a quarto volume of the *Regulations* fully illustrated, which is revised from time to time to conform to new orders and changes.

The arms and equipment of the rank and file have been dealt with in the *List of Changes* first published in 1860, each change being illustrated at first by crude wood engravings but in later years by process blocks.

It is difficult to explain the fact that while many works have

[1] *Creevey Papers*, p. 236.   [2] W.O. 3/328, p. 244.

been produced up to the present dealing with swords of earlier periods or with civilian fencing and duelling, only one author in the last hundred years has dealt specifically and scientifically with the sword as a fighting weapon of modern armies.[1]

It is true that in the middle of the nineteenth century the subject was frequently discussed in Service periodicals, notably by the late General Sir C. Beauchamp Walker, Colonel F. J. Graves, Mr Henry Wilkinson and Mr John Latham; the former being distinguished Cavalry officers, and the last two being authorities of the first order on the manufacture of swords, and on the conditions which rule, or should rule, their design. But from observations of officers evidently interested in the subject, we find that while opinions differed materially on the importance of the sword as a weapon, the majority of writers were agreed that the ideal sword, especially for Cavalry, could never be evolved and that the lance (which was the weapon under special consideration in these Journals) was, when combined with pistol or carbine, the favoured weapon for modern Cavalry operations. Indeed, the late General Brabazon and certain officers of the present day, who had had practical experience in war, have gone so far as to suggest that a combination of the lance and mace, or battle-axe, is the better equipment for Cavalry.[2]

In the latter part of the eighteenth century uniform and equipment was not subject to the definite regulations which rule to-day, and commanding officers had to bear the cost of many items which are now provided out of public funds.

In 1725 it was reported to the War Department that in Colonel Handasyde's Regiment of Foot there were 360 firelocks and bayonets deficient. The Colonel was therefore ordered to replace these from the Ordnance Store at the cost of 24s. per firelock and 2s. per bayonet. In the following year when Colonel Otway transferred two companies from his regiment to

[1] Colonel Marey, *Mémoire sur les Armes Blanches*, 1841.

[2] Maj.-General von Czerlieu (*Journal of the Royal United Service Institution*, XLVII) quotes Seidlitz as in favour of a sword or mace for Cavalry.

that of Colonel Handasyde the latter did not approve of their arms and Colonel Otway had to return them to Store and purchase other arms at a cost of £153.[1]

The arms of the several regiments were therefore the personal property of the Commanding Officer and this arrangement lasted up to the end of the century. A Memorandum from the Horse Guards, dated 27 March 1799, reads as follows: "His Royal Highness is of opinion that as the accoutrements are the personal property of the colonel it would be advisable that you should take those belonging to the 5th Dragoons into your care in preference to lodging them with the Ordnance." This Order is addressed to Major-General Henry Fox, youngest son of the first Lord Holland.[2]

While there was some attempt to standardize weapons the very fact that no State factories existed till well into the nineteenth century made it impossible to lay down hard and fast rules. With the succession of George IV to the throne and the establishment of peace in Europe, the military authorities had an opportunity to set their house in order, a result being the issue of *Dress Regulations*.

Unfortunately there are but few informative records preserved in the War Office papers previous to 1822 which might indicate the reasons for discarding one pattern in favour of another.

In 1884 a *Treatise on Military Small Arms* was produced by Lieut.-Col. H. Bond, R.A., under the aegis of the War Office, which besides technical details gives a short history of the arms of the British Army with some useful illustrations. The next illustrated works are the *Tables of Small Arms* of 1893–1910, and the *Dress Regulations* from 1900 onwards. In the *Tables* all the swords are drawn with the hilt in profile, thus, with the exception of the Scottish broadsword, band-swords and sword-bayonets, making it impossible to recognize the design of most of the Cavalry and staff-sergeants' swords. The design for the Infantry sword of 1895, however, is clearly shown in three

---

[1] W.O. 26/17, pp. 45, 147.   [2] W.O. 3/19, p. 282.

positions in the "Specifications", and the Cavalry 1908 pattern, even when drawn in profile, explains itself sufficiently. The *Dress Regulations* of 1900 and 1911 are more precise as regards the illustrations of officers' swords, for these are mostly shown in profile and in plan, and the swords of Rifle Regiments and the Royal Army Medical Corps are sufficiently well reproduced in three-quarter profile.

In the *Dress Regulations* between the years 1822 and 1904 no dates of approval of the several patterns are given, and in the last-mentioned year, though the date for the General Officer's sword is recorded as 1896 and that of Rifle Regiments as 1902, there is no indication of the fact that these were, in their main designs, the same as the patterns of 1831 and 1822 respectively. For some unexplained reason drawings of officers' swords of the Household Cavalry are omitted from the *Dress Regulations*.

The information given in these volumes from 1822 up to 1894 is disheartening in the extreme, for terms are employed which, although they were understood at the time, convey little or nothing to us at the present day without the supporting evidence of actual examples or illustrations. Such terms as "shell", "boat-shell", or "half-basket" might be employed to describe sword-hilts of many entirely different types, and in the case of earlier patterns it is only by finding weapons dated or ensigned with the Royal monogram, by reference to portraits or to military prints, that we are able to explain the official nomenclature. Here again we are faced with difficulties, for in portraits it may be that the sitter is painted in General's uniform but wearing the sword of his regiment or of an obsolete type.

Modern military artists are serious offenders, for they more often depict the soldier facing to the right with his sword hidden from view, or facing to the left with the sword-hilt obscured by the wearer's hand, or sometimes they shamelessly skimp the drawing of the hilt, proof positive that in the nineteenth century at any rate the artist suffered from that ignorance of the varieties of the regulation sword, which is put forward as one of the reasons for these all too incomplete notes.

Many swords of the eighteenth and nineteenth centuries are still with us in the Tower and in other collections, but when we find them in Mid-Victorian Inventories entered as "80 swords of various nationalities" we cannot hope to obtain useful evidence from records of this nature. It is to contemporary prints and drawings that we have to turn, and at any rate between the years 1742 and 1830 we have records by draughtsmen more or less skilled and, what is more important, the drawings are dated. These taken in conjunction with the vast mass of Army Orders, Inspections and Returns preserved in the Public Record Office, help us with some degree of certainty to date the weapons we possess or reconstruct those missing from the pictorial records.

The earliest of these is the *Representation of Cloathing of His Majesty's Forces*, a volume of coloured engravings made in 1742 to the order of the Duke of Cumberland, of which copies are to be found in Windsor, the War Office and Prince Consort (Aldershot) Libraries, wherein with some degree of clarity the swords and other weapons of Cavalry and Infantry are depicted. The next of importance is the collection of paintings preserved at Windsor Castle by David Morier, a Swiss who was engaged at a salary of £200 per annum by the Duke of Cumberland to make records of the uniforms and equipment of the period, most of his works being dated 1751. Morier's detail in such items as sword-hilt and horse furniture form incontestable evidence of the armament and uniform of the years from 1742 to 1751. For those who cannot journey so far afield there are excellent tracings of Morier's paintings in the War Office Library made by the Rev. P. Sumner, who has made exhaustive studies of military uniforms for over twenty years. The set of coloured engravings by Edward Dayes in the British Museum gives valuable detail respecting the arms of the Infantry in 1792, and it is to be regretted that this artist did not record with the same exactitude of detail the equipment of Cavalry Regiments.

At the beginning of the nineteenth century drastic changes took place in the uniform and equipment of the Army which are recorded by three artists with varying degrees of excellence. Denis Dighton, who had a commission in the 90th Regiment, was made military draughtsman to the Prince of Wales in 1815, and in this position produced records of uniforms and arms which are unequalled in their accuracy of detail, to say nothing of an artistic feeling for design. These drawings, which are dated 1814–17, are preserved in the Library at Windsor Castle. Another military artist of the same period was Lieut.-Col. Charles Hamilton-Smith, D.A.Q.M.G., who seems to have been employed by the War Department as Dighton was employed by Royalty. Hamilton-Smith served in the Army from 1797 to 1820 and therefore had an intimate knowledge of his subject. His albums, preserved in the Victoria and Albert Museum, are filled with sketches of everything that interested this omnivorous artist, ranging from detailed drawings of uniforms to animals, birds, flowers and Indian temples. In 1815 he issued a book of coloured prints under the title *Costume of the Army of the British Empire, according to the last Dress Regulations*, 1814. Smith was a master of detail and the uniform and equipment of the several figures can be quoted as reliable contemporary evidence. A copy of this work is in the Library of the Royal United Services Institution, which also possesses the *Costume of the British Army*, 1828–30, a volume of coloured lithographs by Englemann from drawings by E. Hull. The work here is not so careful as that of Hamilton-Smith, but it is sufficiently detailed to be a guide in essential points.

The student of comparatively modern arms must be warned against taking the sculptor, or indeed the historical painter, as an infallible guide. In statuary the Duke of Wellington at Hyde Park Corner wears a sword which was not regularized till 1831. This was possibly copied from the sword in the Royal United Services Museum which, according to tradition, was carried by the Duke in all his campaigns, at least fifteen years before it was ordered in the *Dress Regulations*. Indeed, Hamilton-Smith's drawing, dated 1814, in the volume above referred to shows a Field-Marshal with an entirely different weapon. When we find that the two infantrymen at the base of Wellington's statue carry *French* flintlock muskets instead of "Brown Bess", we feel that criticism of the historical accuracy of this monument must be charitably withheld. Another offender is the sculptor of the statue of Lord Roberts on the Horse Guards Parade which shows the regulation Field-Marshal's sword in a wide Light Cavalry scabbard which has an enormous "drag", in spite of the fact that the Field-Marshal's regulation scabbard is cut off square with no "drag" at all. One can only surmise that, like Wellington, Roberts was a law unto himself and used whatever scabbard took his fancy and dared the Army Council to criticize.

We will now consider briefly the several aspects of the sword, its functions and its forms from the eleventh century up to the present day and the reasons suggested for the various changes of design.

Royal Cyphers on Swords.

George I–III   George IV   William IV
Victoria   Edward VII   George V
Edward VIII   George VI

The Sword through the Centuries

THE SWORD THROUGH THE CENTURIES

THE SWORD

The sword may be divided into four parts, blade, grip, guard and pommel.

BLADE. This may be straight, curved, or "yataghan", that is, with a slight reverse curve (Fig. 1, 7). The blade is single-edged for cutting only, double-edged for cut and thrust, or with pipe back, that is, a strongly rounded back for thrusting. The point is either the "spear point" which explains itself, or the "hatchet point" set at an obtuse angle to the back and found only on straight cutting swords. The "fullers" are broad shallow grooves on either side of the blade to lighten the weight without decreasing the strength. The blade is divided into "forte", that is, the strongest part where the full force of the cut should come, and "foible", the weakest part near the point. The "tang" is the extension of the blade, which either perforates the grip, and is riveted over the pommel, or is broad and has the grip in two parts riveted on either side.

GRIP. This is generally of wood covered with fishskin bound with twisted wire, or in some cases it consists of two thick pieces of chequered leather riveted on either side of the tang. The grip of the 1908 Cavalry sword is of solid dermatine, and is shaped rather on the lines of the butt of a pistol.

GUARD. There are several types of handguard: the plain cross-guard or "quillons"; the knuckle-bow of one curved bar; the shells flat or boat-shaped which lie at the base of the grip; the three-bar; the basket, an arrangement of trellis-like bars, or in the case of the Highland sword, a combination of bars and small plates; the half-basket which does not completely protect the hand; and the bowl as found on the Cavalry swords of 1899 and 1908.

(15)

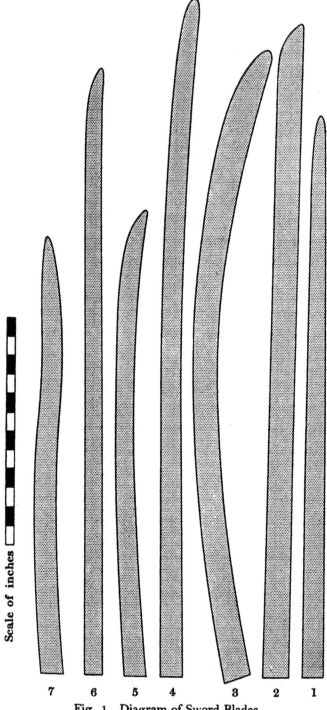

Scale of inches

Fig. 1. Diagram of Sword Blades.

1. Officer, 1790–1822.
2. Heavy Cavalry, 1790–1815.
3. Light Cavalry, 1796–1820.
4. Cavalry, 1834.
5. Infantry "Hanger", 1742–63.
6. Officer and Staff-Sergeant, 1822–95.
7. Sword Bayonet, 1867.

POMMEL. This is the knob or finial at the lower end of the grip through which the tang is riveted, and under which the bars or bowl are attached.

The general attitude towards the sword of the present day is very different from that of the fifteenth and sixteenth centuries, when the knight considered that his weapon was the symbol of his prowess and honour, and as such was deemed worthy of names such as "Excalibur", "Joyeuse" and "Durandel" in token of his personal affection. The only nation which still preserves this cult is the Japanese, to whom even the modern Service sword is an object of profound veneration. As an instance of this may be quoted a circumstance which came under personal notice at the beginning of the War of 1914–18, when a Japanese officer was inspecting the superb sword-blade made by Masamatsu in the year 1390, deposited in the Tower Armouries by the late Lord Kitchener's Trustees. On being asked if he would like to handle the blade, the officer covered his hands with a handkerchief and as he received it he sprang to attention and raised the sword to eye-level. That same day a number of British Service swords were noticed reposing in the umbrella rack at one of our Service Clubs.[1] It may be that the reason for this neglect of the sword is threefold, in that the modern weapon is not decorative, nor is it a convenient symbol of office, nor, with one notable exception, is it a practical weapon of offence. It has therefore come to be considered as a useless item of equipment to be dispensed with on the first opportunity.

Now there are two essential factors to be observed in all products of craftsmanship, without which the object under consideration can never be treated seriously. First of these is suitability of purpose for which the object is intended, and the second is convenience in use. Under the heading of Suitability of Purpose it will be obvious that the sole function of a sword is that of a fighting weapon. It will therefore be necessary to con-

[1] The Japanese Infantry officer still carries a two-hand sword in action.

sider how this has been achieved in the different patterns adopted during the last hundred years.

Primarily the purpose of the sword is as a weapon of offence and secondly as a guard. From the thirteenth century onwards most types of swords failed notably in both these factors. The so-called "Crusader" sword is heavy, broad-bladed and short-gripped. There is no balance, as the word is understood in swordsmanship, and to thrust with it is an impossibility, though the sharpened point suggests that such an action might be intended. It could only be used for a sweeping cut and its weight made swift recovery impossible. This, however, was not essential as the swordsman used his shield as a guard. The Elizabethan rapier was more practicable for cut and thrust, but, on account of its length, in later years it was of little value at close quarters and could only be usefully employed in a duel, or single combat, but never in battle.

It would seem to be advisable to classify the functions of swords under the three headings: Thrusting, Cutting, and Cut and Thrust.

All authorities consider that thrusting with the sword is more effectual and that the wounds thus produced are more difficult to heal than those from a cut, and all agree that the thrusting sword is the better for Cavalry, and in some respects also for Infantry. Some officers, however, in recent years have pointed out that though the use of the point is essential in the charge, it cannot be used in close-quarter mêlée and that a man must cut his way out.[1] The main objection to the cutting weapon is that except in the case of the expert swordsman the tendency in moments of excitement is to cut wildly, more often with the flat, than with the edge leading.[2] Lord Wolseley, in commenting on the swords submitted to the 1885 (Drury-Lowe) Com-

[1] Gen. Sir C. Beauchamp Walker, *Journal of the Royal United Service Institution*, XXXIII, 766.
[2] J. Latham, "The Shape of Sword Blades", *Journal of the Royal United Service Institution*, VI, 410–22.

mittee, stated that in his opinion it was wellnigh impossible to produce a sword that would be equally good for cutting and thrusting.

Colonel Marey,[1] the only writer who has treated the subject from a scientific point of view, advises the straight sword for Cavalry and a sword based on the "yataghan" for Infantry (Fig. 1, 7).

Troopers' swords of the Household Cavalry and of Heavy Cavalry in the late eighteenth and early nineteenth centuries were in many respects unsatisfactory as weapons. They were broad-bladed with hatchet-point of no use in thrusting and could only be employed for a heavy cut, which would of course leave the Trooper entirely unguarded, as he would have no time to recover. The Light Cavalry curved sword, however, of the same period, based on the Oriental scimitar, was, if properly used, as good a cutting weapon as could possibly be devised. Its terrific wounding power was frequently noted in the Indian wars of the early nineteenth century, and there is a legend that Napoleon's generals in the Peninsula protested to the Duke of Wellington against the weapon as being too barbarous.[2] Those who, in adopting the Light Cavalry sword, provided only a knuckle-guard, would appear to have ignored the fact that the Oriental cavalryman, armed with scimitar, also used a small shield or an arm defence for guarding. It is strange that after the very strong opinions expressed by Prince Maurice of Saxe[3] and other authorities on the value of the thrusting sword, both the Heavy and Light Cavalry sword of the early nineteenth century should have been solely adopted for cutting. Staff-Sergeant-Major Williams, Inspector of Fencing, asks: "Is the cut of any use to Cavalry?" and answers decidedly "No", and states that only two Russian gunners at Balaklava were killed by sword cuts.[4]

[1] *Mémoire sur les Armes Blanches.*
[2] *History of the 16th Light Dragoons*, I, 245.
[3] Marshal Saxe, *Les Rêveries*, 1756.
[4] *Cavalry Journal*, vol. I.

On the other hand, Colonel H. J. Landon agrees with General Jacob as to the cut being far more effective, and instances an occasion when he was almost pulled out of the saddle by piercing his opponent up to the hilt, with consequent difficulty of recovering his sword. He prefers a straight thrusting sword for Infantry and a curved cutting sword for Cavalry.[1] The same objections may be made to the Highland broadsword, erroneously called the "claymore", for this is entirely a cutting weapon and a thrust is a matter of great difficulty, indeed it is almost an impossibility. The early Highland warriors always employed either a targe, with the dirk held point uppermost in the same hand for thrusting, or the dirk only for thrusting and guard as well.[2]

After these somewhat severe strictures it is pleasant to be able to record that in the modern Cavalry sword we have the finest thrusting weapon which has ever been devised in the whole history of the sword.

We come now to guards. Those of the early nineteenth-century swords are, as often as not, of brass, the Infantry officer's guard from 1822 to 1895 being of open-work pattern, which but meagrely protected the hand and was very liable to be broken or bent. Both the Heavy and Light Cavalry guards of the early nineteenth century were simply knuckle-bows, and as such hardly covered the hand at all. These guards were improved for the Cavalry in the middle of the nineteenth century and from thence onwards the hand has been sufficiently protected.

The second essential referred to above is Convenience in Use, and under this heading the form of the grip is all important. Colonel Marey holds that the grip should be narrower in width across than it is from front to back, and easy and convenient to hold. This pattern is fairly practical in most swords until we come to the Cavalry swords from about 1860 to 1899, when the

---

[1] *Cavalry Journal*, vol. II.

[2] In vol. VI of the *Journal of the Royal United Service Institution*, p. 422, is a note that Admiral Lord Cochrane armed his boarding party with a cutlass and with a bayonet strapped to their left arm as a guard.

grip was almost circular in section and, according to some authorities, most inconvenient to use when the hand was hot, making a cut, with the edge leading, difficult, if not impossible. Marey advocates the hand-stop at the top of the guard, which was employed in the Cavalry swords from about 1860 to 1899, and also speaks very strongly of the position of the thumb. While he does not mention its position in thrusting, he states very strongly that the thumb should *never* be at the back of the grip when cutting, and his remarks suggest that for a cut and thrust sword the position of the thumb would have to be moved. On British swords of recent date it is evident that the thrust is considered the more important action of the two, for most of the grips are chequered at the back, and the present Cavalry sword has a distinct depression for the thumb. This position of the thumb was carried to rather an extreme point in experimental swords of the 1890 pattern, which were altered by inserting a small bowl in front of the handguard to take the thumb and to protect it, while in the experimental pattern submitted to the Committee, a hole was cut out in the front of the guard with the intention that the thumb should go through it. It need hardly be added that this particular sword was rejected as most inconvenient, not to say dangerous, by all the Cavalry Brigades which tested it.

The position of the sword-knot is also of some importance, and Colonel Marey deprecates very much the attachment of the sword-knot near the pommel, stating that it should be attached at the lower part of the guard, for in the former position he considered it was a serious inconvenience to the hand; but de Brac goes still further, and advises the abolition of the sword-knot for service use, and considers that a handkerchief is better.[1] Mention has been made before of the outstanding virtue of the present British Cavalry sword, and we need only add that as a thrusting sword its balance and convenience could not be surpassed. The most inexperienced tyro on being shown how to

---

[1] A. F. de Brac, *Avant-postes de Cavalerie Légère*, 1834.

hold the sword cannot help but come to the "engage" position at once, so admirably is the grip designed. Major Poore, who was a member of the Committee which produced the 1908 Cavalry sword, was, naturally, an enthusiastic champion of the new pistol-shaped grip, but he is somewhat strongly criticized by Major Crichton, who preferred the old pattern Cavalry sword as more useful for cut, thrust and guard.[1]

In considering convenience in use the scabbard must not be left out of consideration. Writing in 1869[2] Colonel Denison urged the use of a wooden lining, as the sword edge coming in contact with the metal scabbard tended to become blunted, and he instances the universal use of the wooden scabbard by Oriental swordsmen in support of his contention. He also recommends the use of fixed loops instead of loose rings, in order to minimize the rattle of accoutrements. As a matter of fact the wood lining had been adopted in the scabbard of the 1864 Cavalry sword, possibly on Denison's suggestion, but the fixed rings were not introduced till 1882.

It is most unfortunate that all detailed records of changes and of the introduction of new patterns prior to about 1884 have been destroyed and we have only succinct references in Army Orders and the *List of Changes* from 1860 to guide our researches. The latter are fairly informative and are of course useful in recognizing an actual pattern or change of pattern. But it is the loss of all records of early committees which is most regrettable, for it is only from these that we could learn the reasons put forward for the introduction of entirely new weapons. In 1885, however, we find reports of committees published in Command Papers which give many interesting details and criticisms which are worthy of more than passing notice as leading up to the introduction of the present Cavalry sword, the only sword which is seriously considered to-day as a fighting weapon.

[1] *Cavalry Journal*, vi, 190, 417.
[2] *Modern Cavalry*.

In 1884 the supply of swords and bayonets for the Army was unsatisfactory in the extreme; for the Egyptian War was in progress and the Government factory at Enfield was employed to the full extent of its power. As far back as 1844[1] the Ordnance had taken over the manufacture of Cavalry swords and this had put many old-established firms out of business and as a result there were few factories in this country which could undertake this highly specialized work to any considerable extent. Orders therefore had to be placed with Solingen firms, who, it must be admitted with regret, had supplied swords for the British Army for over a hundred years. It was reported that many of the swords and bayonets used in Egypt were not only useless but were a positive source of danger to our men; swords were bent by falling horses and instances were given of weapons actually breaking in hand-to-hand combat. One of the principal difficulties appears to have been the methods of tempering which made testing and inspection complicated. It was found in the case of bayonets that as their weight was over regulation standard they were ground down, thereby destroying the "case hardening" favoured in Germany and exposing the soft metal underneath. Criticism raged in the Press and in Parliament for two years and eventually a Committee was appointed to review the whole subject, composed as follows: Major-General Sir D. C. Drury Lowe (President), Sir A. F. Abel (Chemist to the War Department), Colonel H. T. Arbuthnot (Royal Small Arms Factory), Colonel E. A. Wood (10th Hussars), Major C. F. Call (India Store Department), J. F. Latham, Esq. (representing the firm of Wilkinson and Son), J. F. Mappin, Esq. and G. R. Hunt, Esq. (Secretary).

In the course of evidence taken before the Committee it was stated that one of the Solingen Cavalry swords when submitted to the vertical press was bent to an angle of 45° and remained at this angle when taken out of the press. It was suggested by a witness that it was better to have one's sword bent in battle than

---

[1] War Office Circular Letter, 7 March 1844.

broken, as in the former case it could be straightened for further use!

The deliberations of the Committee dragged on for months but little satisfactory progress was made, though it is probable that the methods of manufacture were improved. It stands to reason that it must have been considered undesirable to introduce entirely new weapons to an army in the midst of a campaign in which close-quarter fighting was a matter of everyday occurrence.[1]

With the end of the first Egyptian War the controversy languished, but broke out again in 1889 when a Command Paper on the subject was presented to Parliament,[2] and eventually a sword known as the "1899 pattern" was sealed for Cavalry with a large bowl-shaped handguard.

In 1903 a second Committee was set up to consider the subject on more scientific lines than had been the case previously, and the following Cavalry officers were appointed to serve: General Sir John French (Chairman), Major-General Douglas Haig, Brigadier-General M. F. Rimington and Major-General H. J. Scobell. The Committee rightly considered that the existing Cavalry sword was clumsy and that "whereas a soldier inflicted little bodily injury with a cut, a thrust was always far more effective", a doctrine insisted upon by all authorities from Marshal Saxe onwards. They considered that the "Italian thrust" was to be the method of attack to be aimed at, and working on these lines 200 experimental swords were made and issued to Cavalry commanders for trial and report.

Captain Hutton, the noted fencer, and Colonel the Hon. T. S. Napier (Inspector of Gymnasia) reported adversely on all the swords submitted as not up to requirements and the matter appears to have been dropped.

In 1906 a new Committee was set up composed as follows: Major-General H. J. Scobell (Chairman), Major J. B. Jardine,

[1] War Office Report of Committee on Swords, 1885.
[2] Command Paper c. 5633.

Major E. S. Tickell, Major J. A. Bell-Smythe, Major R. M. Poore, Major A. L. Powell (all Cavalry officers); Colonel G. M. Fox (Chief Inspector of Physical Training, Board of Education), Captain A. Hutton with Captain S. W. Douglas, R.A. and Major W. E. Edwards, R.A. (Secretaries).

The Committee decided that the primary object was to produce a thrusting sword, capable also, if possible, of cutting, and that the reach of the sword should be identical with that of the lance at the "engage". Experimental swords were ordered from Messrs Wilkinson and Messrs Mole, based on the following figures: weight 2 lb. 6 oz.; blade 35 in., with narrow chisel edge; balance $2\frac{1}{2}$–$2\frac{3}{4}$ in. from the hilt, the handle to be shaped to the hand so that there should only be one possible way of holding the sword. The swords before the Committee for testing were those of the Household Cavalry 1892, the Cavalry 1899 and the 1890 converted, the French Cavalry 1854, the French Light Cavalry 1822, a Dutch sword and a Spanish bullfighter's sword. The 1899 sword was tried with a narrow thrusting blade and also with a thumb-hole in the forward part of the guard, intended to keep the hand in the thrusting position, but this was unfavourably reported on as the edge of the hole cut glove and thumb, and the hole itself provided an opening for enemy sword, lance or bayonet. The grip appears to have been designed by Colonel G. M. Fox, who experimented with soft gutta-percha till he produced the present "pistol-grip" pattern.

This grip was tried with the 1899 curved and with the 1904 straight blades, and grips of aluminium, vulcanite and wood were submitted before "dermatine" was decided upon. It was eventually adopted as the 1906 pattern and after several minor alterations were made it was sealed as the 1908 pattern.

Captain Hutton at first condemned the new sword and suggested that the 1899 grip made with octagonal section should be adopted, and Colonel the Hon. J. S. Napier, who had previously condemned the experiments of the 1903 Committee, disapproved of the thrusting sword, giving as his opinion that the soldier's first need was to cut and that as the cutting sword had been the favoured weapon for 500 years it must of necessity be the weapon of the future.

Eventually Captain Hutton recorded a somewhat qualified approval, stating that while the sword was good for the thrust, it should also be possible to make it a cutting weapon, a desideratum which, Captain Hutton's lifelong study of the sword of all ages should have shown him, had never been achieved by the most skilled swordsmith of any country or century. At last the sword as we know it to-day was passed, and was submitted to King Edward who, while he criticized the design of the hilt, was impressed by the practical advantages of the sword as a fighting weapon and gave his approval on 2 July 1908.

It is this sword, with slight modifications, which is carried to-day by the British Cavalry, and with smaller hilt and grip in the Indian Army by those regiments which do not wear the tulwar. The officer's sword of similar pattern but with decorated hand-guard was approved in 1913.

The *Dress Regulations* of 1934 lay down that "swords will be carried on active service and in 'Marching order' by officers serving in Cavalry regiments only". The result of this order is that swords of all other arms of the Service disappear as fighting weapons.

Certain of the earlier types of weapons have disappeared, but as far as has been possible, representative exhibits of those used in the British Army from the Restoration up to the present day are to be found in the Armouries of the Tower and in the Imperial War Museum.

Swords of the Army

WITH A NOTE ON NAVAL SWORDS

SWORDS OF THE ARMY

GENERAL OFFICERS

From the beginning of the eighteenth century General Officers carried the simple straight sword with knuckle-bow and shells like that of the officers of Cavalry and Infantry (Plate II, 1). In the engraving in the *British Military Library* of 1799 the Prince of Wales (George IV) is depicted as the Commander-in-Chief, surrounded by his Staff wearing this sword and therefore, presumably, dressed according to the Regulations then in force.

A minute dated Horse Guards 18 March 1803 states that: "A pattern sword for officers of Grenadiers and Light Infantry has been approved by His Majesty to-gether with the pattern sword for Regimental Officers of Infantry and for the General Staff of the Army. The Mounted Officers of Flank Companies use the same sword belt and carry their swords in the same manner as other Regimental Officers. The Officers of the General Staff use the waist-belt."[1] This sword is shown in a portrait of General Charles Leigh by Loutherbourg and the sealed pattern is exhibited in the Armouries of the Tower. General Leigh was promoted General in 1803 and must have been one of the first officers to carry the new sword (Plate II, 2).

Fig. 2. General Officer, 1803.

The earliest illustrations of General Officers are to be found in Hamilton-Smith's book of lithographs[2] which is described on the title-page as "According to the last *Dress Regulations* of 1814". Here the Field-Marshal is

[1] W.O. 3/35, p. 462.
[2] *Costume of the Army of the British Empire*, 1815.

shown with what we assume to be a "boat-shell" hilt (Plate II, 3) which is entirely different from the hilt of 1799 referred to above. Generals, on the other hand, are shown with the sword-hilt of the 1799 pattern which was ordered in General Order 4 May 1796. Up to the time of writing the *Dress Regulations* of 1814 have not been discovered, but even if they were known, it is probable that the descriptions are vague in the extreme. The statue of George III by Matthew Wyatt erected in 1836 in Cockspur Street shows a true "boat-shell" hilt, presumably copied from the King's own sword of 1814 which very properly conformed to Regulations. There must have been some misunderstanding on the matter, or what is more possible, the General Officers disregarded the order, for the first printed *Regulations* of 1816 deal only with General Officers, omitting all mention of Field-Marshals and the rest of the Army. These new orders describe the hilt as "gilt with shells", which may certainly be said to describe the 1814 pattern, but it is also used to describe the simpler Infantry officer's sword in the *Dress Regulations* of 1822. It is possible that Field-Marshals were omitted from the 1816 *Regulations* because they were all members of the Royal Family excepting Wellington, who received the baton in 1813. The Duke seems to have been a law unto himself as regards swords, for all his portraits show weapons of various designs but none of them of regulation pattern. He is generally painted with a "Mameluke"[1] hilted sword, a type which was not regularized till the *Regulations* of 1831. There is a sword of this design exhibited in the Royal United Services Museum which is labelled as carried by him in all his campaigns.

The *Regulations* of 1822 order a hilt of entirely different design and identical with the Infantry officer's "Gothic" hilt of

---

[1] The Mamelukes were a body of white slaves enrolled in Egypt as the Sultan's bodyguard. In 1250 their leader overthrew the government and made himself Sultan of Egypt. They were exterminated by Mehemet Ali in 1811.

the same date (Plate II, 4). The Tower possesses the sword of Frederick Augustus, Duke of York, of this Gothic pattern, but it is somewhat perplexing to find that instead of the crossed batons of a Field-Marshal, the Duke of York's sword bears only the crossed baton and sword, the badge of a Lieutenant-General, in spite of the fact that the Duke had been a Field-Marshal since 1795.

The whole of this study of swords is complicated and disturbing in the extreme, especially when drastic alterations are made and no explanatory reason is forthcoming. From about the middle of the eighteenth century all officers, including those of the highest rank, carried swords of the same pattern and the 1822 sword is the last to follow this ruling. It was possibly due to the Duke of Wellington that the sword which he had carried, in spite of definite regulations, was adopted for Field-Marshals and Generals in 1831, a pattern which is still in use at the present day (Plate II, 5). In the *Dress Regulations* of 1934, para. 204, it is ordered that Field-Marshals and Generals on active service should wear the sword of the arm from which the officer was promoted.

HOUSEHOLD CAVALRY

To describe with clarity the arms of the Household Cavalry it is necessary first to record the changes which have taken place in the organization of the Royal mounted bodyguard. After the Restoration certain gentlemen were enrolled as the Sovereign's personal guard and these were styled Life or Horse Guards, both terms being used in contemporary accounts.

In addition two troops of Horse Grenadiers were raised in 1693, copied from the Grenadiers à Cheval, raised by Louis XIV in 1676. In 1750 all units of the Royal bodyguard were styled Horse Guards and were composed of four regiments. In 1788, by Royal Warrant of 8 June, a sweeping change was made in their organization.

The 1st and 2nd Horse Guards continued in being, the 3rd

and 4th were disbanded, while the Horse Grenadiers were disbanded and re-enlisted as the 1st and 2nd Life Guards.

Mounted units or "Horse" were equipped with helmet, breast and back plates as late as 13 February 1677/8, but this body armour must have been given up by 1690 when the Armourers of London presented a petition to Parliament in which they state that "armour is no longer worn by Horse and Foot and their trade is thereby ruined".[1]

The helmet alone survived, as we learn from one of Colonel St Pierre's letters in 1707. He writes: "My Lord has also got iron scull caps for the Dragoons."[2] Grose, writing in 1786, says that these were worn "these twenty or thirty years", that is, about 1750.[3] It is possible that he refers to "Secrete", a spider-like iron lining to the felt hats, of which large numbers were returned to the Tower in the eighteenth century.

We shall refer later to the arms and exercises of the rank and file and shall deal in the first place with the swords of the officers.

As has been pointed out in the Introduction, we are entirely dependent on signed and dated portraits, sketches and engravings for determining the date of any particular weapon, as it is seldom that the weapon itself bears any inscription or date. We must therefore be guided by these pictorial records in putting forward our suppositions.

OFFICERS

As far as can be gathered from these sources all officers of Horse or Foot carried the straight sword with gilt knuckle-bow and shells as shown on Plate II, 1; fig. 49, the Cavalry blade being heavier than that of the Infantry weapon.

The earliest pictorial records of officers' swords are to be

[1] Proceedings of the House of Commons, 11 November 1690.
[2] Brit. Mus. Add. MSS. 31134, p. 422.
[3] *Military Antiquities*, II, 243.

found in the series of careful drawings of Denis Dighton preserved in the Library at Windsor Castle.

Dighton made sketches and minutely finished water-colour drawings of the uniform and equipment of officers of the Life Guards and Horse Guards, each dated between the years 1814 and 1820, which give beyond all doubt the officer's sword of the period. Both regiments are shown as wearing a straight broad-bladed sword with a true basket-hilt of gilt bars, on the outer side of which is a large escutcheon bearing the Royal Crest, a lion upon a crown (Fig. 3).

Fig. 3. Household Cavalry
Officer, 1814.

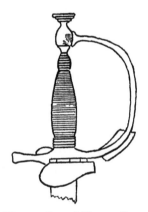

Fig. 4. Royal Horse Guards
Officer (Dress), 1822.

On the accession of George IV *Dress Regulations* dated 1822 were issued in which drastic alterations were made, and as these are somewhat complicated it will be advisable to take each pattern of sword separately. Three swords of different types were ordered for the 1st and 2nd Life Guards as follows:

Full Dress. Pommel, urn-shaped; grip, fishskin bound with gilt wire; guard, boat-shell, all gilt; blade, straight 32 × 1 in.; scabbard, brass with inlets of fishskin.

Dress. Guard, half-basket and shells, gilt; blade, straight 34 × 1 in.; scabbard, black leather with gilt mounts.

Undress. As Dress, but with open shell-guard and slightly curved blade with "pipe back" 36 in.

The Royal Horse Guards carried swords which are described as follows:

Full Dress. Pommel, urn-shaped, knuckle-bow and boat-shells all gilt; blade, straight 32 × 1 in.; scabbard of steel (Plate II, 6; fig. 4).

Dress and Undress. The hilt is the same, but whereas the grip of Full Dress sword is bound with silver wire that of the Dress sword is bound with yellow wire. The blade and scabbard of the Dress sword are the same as that of the Full Dress, while the blade of both swords is 34½ in. and the scabbard brass with fishskin inlets.

With regard to the Full Dress hilt of the Life Guards we are faced with the vague description which will be referred to frequently in these pages.

What was this "half-basket with shells"? We can only assume, and we trust we are right in our conjecture, that unjustifiable extravagance was not aimed at and that the hilt of 1814–20 above referred to was regularized at any rate for the Life Guards. At the same time it is remarkable that the elaborate escutcheon on the guard is not mentioned. What is indeed surprising is that officers of both the Life Guards and Horse Guards were ordered three entirely different types of sword for various occasions each with a blade of different pattern. The Horse Guards were distinct from the Life Guards as to swords, as their hilts, at any rate from the official description, are different in every detail.

Following the example of his predecessor, William IV issued new *Dress Regulations* in 1834 and, evidently impressed by the openly expressed discontent at the extravagance of the former reign, abolished the three types of sword in favour of one pattern. But, strange to relate, whereas formerly the two regiments of Life Guards had carried the same swords, in the new

Regulations they were ordered entirely different patterns. For the 1st Life Guards the sword was as follows:

Pommel of brass, stepped; grip, fishskin bound silver wire; guard, steel with 12 brass studs on margin with pierced design and small brass ornaments with 1.L.G. in brass applied, the whole lined with white buckskin. The blade with hatchet point was $40 \times 1\frac{1}{2}$ in. and the scabbard of steel with brass mounts (Plate II, 7; fig. 5).

For the 2nd Regiment the pommel was chased, the grip bound with brass wire and the guard of three chased and scrolled bars, the "stool" being ornamented on both sides with a grenade. The blade, the longest of any Service issue, was $40 \times 1\frac{1}{2}$ in. and the scabbard of steel with reeded brass mounts.

The Royal Horse Guards apparently carried on the "boat-shell" hilt of the former regulations, but in place of a 34-in. blade carried one of 39×1 in.

Here is another conundrum to be solved. Is the hilt of bars with ornamented "stool" a revival of the 1814 pattern copied from the sword of the French Horse Grenadiers, the grenade being possibly a reminder that the Life Guards sprang from the disbanded Horse Grenadiers of 1788? The solution seems to rest with the meaning of the word "stool". Burn, in his *French-English Naval and Military Dictionary*, 1854, explains the word as the "shell" or *coquille* of the sword which in the military vocabulary of 1834 may be the escutcheon above referred to. Be this as it may, this sword with a grenade on the hilt is unknown in illustrations or in actual examples, so that it is pos-

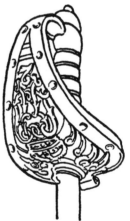

Fig. 5. 1st Life Guards Officer, 1834.
1st and 2nd Life Guards Officer, 1874.

sible that the old 1814 sword was used and the Royal Crest allowed in defiance of all regulations. The Household Cavalry officers had financial respite till 1874, when the *Dress Regulations* realize the confusion of these different patterns and order one sword for all officers of the Household Cavalry, based on the more or less practical weapon of the 1st Life Guards of 1834, the guard bearing 1.L.G., 2.L.G. and R.H.G. in brass with a blade 30 × $1\frac{1}{8}$ in. This sword is still in use for ceremonial purposes (Plate II, 7; figs. 5, 6).

Fig. 6. Monograms on Household Cavalry handguards, 1834 to present day.

The Service sword is the same as that of the Cavalry pattern 1908 which will be described in detail on p. 55, the regimental monograms and numbers being engraved on the handguard. The only difference is on the pommel; that of the Life Guards being stepped and of the Horse Guards oval chequered. The 1911 *Dress Regulations* leave the space for text and illustration blank as the new sword was not ordered till 1912.

TROOPER[1]

The chief sources from which we draw our information are the *Representation of Cloathing of His Majesty's Forces*, 1742, a volume of coloured engravings in the Windsor, War Office and Prince Consort (Aldershot) Libraries, and the paintings, dated 1751, by David Morier at Windsor Castle. In the earlier

---

[1] As the terms Trooper and Private are both used in contemporary records it is considered simpler to use the former which has for authority *King's Regulations*, 1935, para. 267, Sec. IV.

SWORD HILTS; Plates II–III

1. All officers 1750–1800. 2. General officers and Guards 1803. 3. General officers 1814. 4. General officers 1822. 5. General officers 1831. 6. Life Guards officer 1822. 7. Household Cavalry officer 1834. 8. Household Cavalry officer (service) 1912. 9. Horse Guards trooper 1742. 10. (?) Horse and Dragoon trooper 1751. 11. (?) Household Cavalry trooper 1796. 12. Horse Guards and Heavy Cavalry trooper 1807. 13. Life Guards trooper 1829. 14. Household Cavalry 1882. 15. Dragoon officer 1742. 16. Heavy Cavalry 1834. 17. Heavy Cavalry officer and Royal Engineers 1857. 18. Cavalry officer 1896. 19. Heavy Cavalry trooper 1830. 20. Cavalry trooper 1853. 21 Cavalry trooper 1864. 22. Cavalry trooper 1899. 23. Cavalry trooper 1908. 24. Light Infantry trooper 1796. 25. Royal Artillery and Light Cavalry officer 1822. 26. Infantry officer 1750. 27. Guards, Flank company 1803. 28. Infantry officer 1822. 29. Infantry officer 1895. 30. Infantry private 1742. 31. Grenadier 1751. 32. Highland broad-sword. 33. Pioneer 1856–1903. 34. Land Transport 1855–7. 35. Band 1829. 36. Drummer 1840. 37. Drummer 1895. 38. Plug bayonet 1663–1700. 39. Serjeant's halberd 1670–1800. 40. Serjeant's spontoon 1800–30.

PLATE II

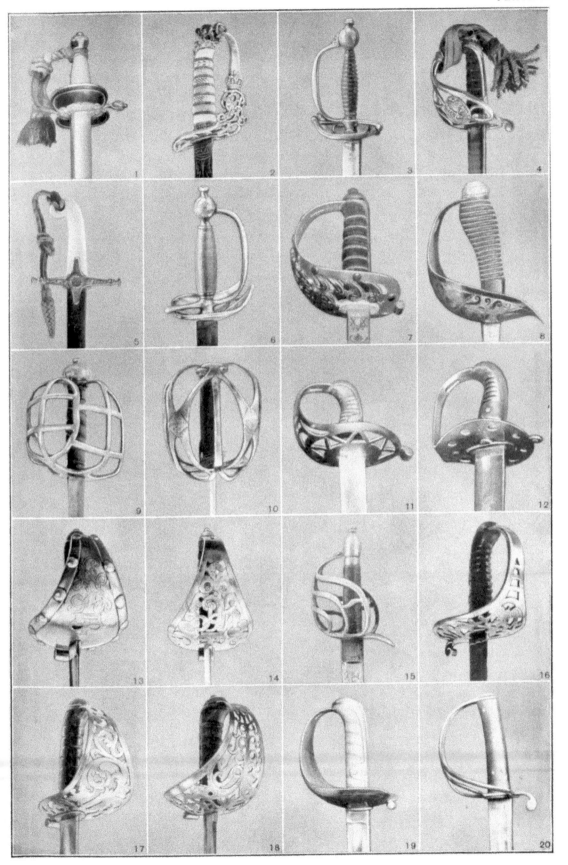

PLATE III

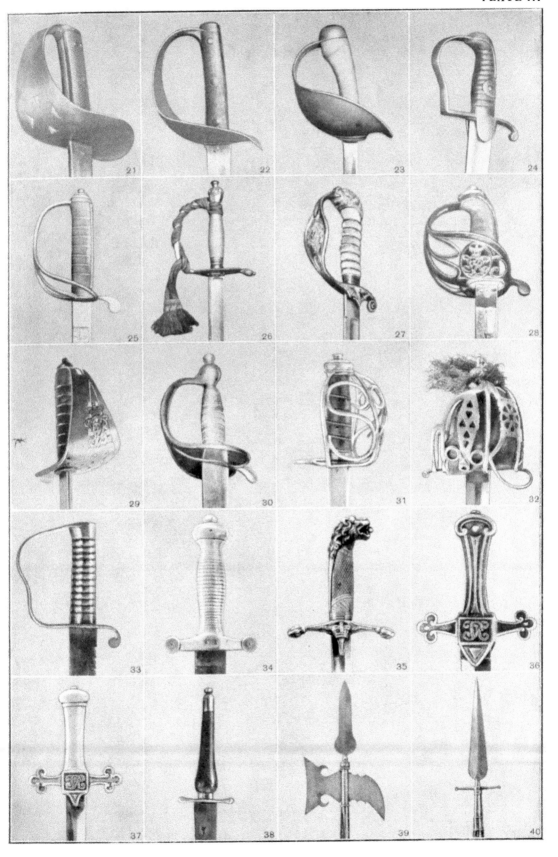

volume the figures are coloured and the details for the most part have the air of accuracy. The artist is unknown but the production of these volumes is ascribed to the efforts of William Augustus, Duke of Cumberland to hand down to posterity the uniforms then worn in the British Army.

Before dealing in detail with these two records it will be necessary to give a brief account of the equipment and arms carried by the Cavalry. These were sword, pistols, musket and bayonet, ammunition and, in the case of Horse Grenadiers, a pouch of grenades.

The drill or "Exercise" was somewhat complicated, for it should be remembered that each man had a large and heavy hat, great boots, uniform overlaid with cross-belts, sword, pistol-holsters and a musket carried in a bucket and slung over the right leg. For the Heavy Cavalry we may take the *Exercise for Horse, Dragoons and Foot Forces* of 1739 as typical and in this are 180 orders for a troop on going into action. These may be epitomized as follows: The troop is drawn up in order of battle with drawn swords and the exercise continues: Return swords, pull off gloves, sling firelock, dismount, link horses, have a care, present, fire, reload, fix bayonets, unfix bayonets, unlink horses, mount, draw swords. These are embodied in 138 orders, the remaining 42 being evolutions.

For the Horse Grenadiers we must go back to an earlier record, the *Abridgment of Military Discipline*, 1686, in the days when the plug-bayonet was in use and when, obviously, the musket could not be fired with the bayonet fixed. Here the same proceeding is followed but the Grenadier having fired, fixed bayonet, charged, unfixed bayonet and fired again; threw his grenades, retired, fell in "with a huzza", slung his musket, unlinked horses and remounted and again fired his musket. One can but wonder what action the enemy was taking in the meantime. As a matter of fact he was probably going through very similar "Exercises" on his own account.

The muskets or fusils as they are often called were much the same as those carried by the Infantry, and as no written records exist of these as used by the Household Cavalry we shall consider their use in fuller detail under the heading of Cavalry on pp. 43, 130.

The swords shown in the *Representation of Cloathing* have the true basket-hilt, and according to the colouring of the plates those of the 1st, 3rd and 4th Regiments of Horse Guards were of brass and of the 2nd Regiment of steel (Plate II, 9; fig. 7). The

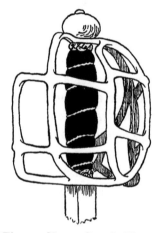

Fig. 7. Horse Guards Trooper, 1742–51.

Fig. 8. 1st Horse Guards Trooper, 1751.

blade was apparently straight and heavy for cutting and of no use for thrusting.

The Royal Regiment or "Oxford Blues", together with the regiments of Horse and of Dragoons, all carried the true Highland broadsword hilt and this type of sword was worn by the Cavalry as early as 1706 (Plate II, 10; fig. 12).[1]

Our next record is the collection of David Morier's paintings at Windsor dated 1751 and here we find certain changes. The troopers still carry muskets and bayonets, but the 1st Regiment of Horse Guards have a simpler brass-hilted sword (Fig. 8) while the 2nd Regiment continue to carry the former pattern.

[1] A.O. 17/28, p. 154.

On 14 November 1796 a new sword was issued to the Horse Guards,[1] but no details are given and up to the time of writing no pictorial record has been found to give us the design. In the Tower Stores a number of swords have been preserved which for about a hundred years or more have been listed as Life Guards' swords. They are straight broad-bladed weapons with large brass handguards pierced with geometrical patterns, unquestionably English, for many of them are marked CRAVEN and WOOLEY DEAKIN (Plate II, 11; fig. 9). The frog-hooks of the brass scabbards prove that they were carried on a cross-belt and not on slings. The guards and scabbards are of soft brass and will not stand ordinary hard usage, let alone the strain of battle. It is possible, indeed probable, that these may be dated about 1796 and that owing to their constructional weakness the whole issue was withdrawn for a more serviceable weapon, and that as they were brass and not steel they were sent to the Tower

Fig. 9. Household Cavalry Trooper, ? 1796–1807.

for decorative purposes and not remade to suit new conditions.

A drawing in Lieut.-Col. Hamilton-Smith's "Commonplace" book in the Victoria and Albert Museum shows a careful representation, undated, of a Private in the "Oxford Blues", now the Royal Horse Guards, with what we know as the "disk" hilt, and a similar sword is shown on a sketch of the Scots Greys, dated 1807. Hamilton-Smith's coloured lithos in his costly volume[2] show the same sword-hilt but with lesser detail for the 1st Life Guards, described as the "New Pattern Uniform", for the Horse Guards, the Greys and for the 3rd Dragoons; all these prints being dated 1815 (Plate II, 12; fig. 17). In these illustrations

[1] W.O. 3/15, p. 263.
[2] *Costume of the Army of the British Empire*, 1815.

both officers and troopers of the Household Cavalry are shown with the sabretache. If the brass-hilted swords were ever issued they were certainly abolished before 1807, when the Household Cavalry privates carried the same sword as did the Heavy Cavalry. This type of sword is shown in Colonel John Luard's *History of the Dress of the British Soldier* under the date 1760, but this must not be taken as evidence, so far as the British Army is concerned. The pattern was copied from an Austrian Heavy Cavalry sword of the last years of the eighteenth century. As the name implies, the hilt has a simple knuckle-bow, a large disk pierced with holes at the base of the grip. The blade is single-edged with hatchet point.

The hilt illustrated in Plate II, 13 and fig. 10 is given, but without very clear detail, in Hull and Englemann's coloured lithographs of 1829.[1] The swords are plainly shown, but owing to the small size of the print the engraved monogram is missed. It would appear therefore that this sword was ordered for troopers shortly after the *Dress Regulations* for officers were issued in 1822 and that the same design but more ornate was laid down for the officers in the *Regulations* of 1834.

Fig. 10.   1st Life Guards Trooper, 1829.

The War Office *List of Changes* begins in 1860 and here at last we are on surer ground, but although we obtain definite information as to the length of blade, weight, etc., it is some years before we are favoured with illustrations and these, as often as not, are not very informative. A series of line photo-prints was issued from time to time, the last date including the 1908 Cavalry sword, but in the majority of cases the sword-hilts are shown in profile and therefore are not readily identifiable. In 1882[2]

---

[1] *Costume of the British Army*, 1828–30.
[2] *List of Changes*, 4052.

two new-pattern swords were issued to the Household Cavalry, both scheduled as Mark I, a long straight blade $38\frac{7}{8}$ in. and a short blade, for use by the band, $34\frac{7}{8}$ in. The hilt is of sheet steel, pierced with scroll-work and H.C. (Plate II, 14; fig. 11). In

Fig. 11. Household Cavalry Trooper, 1882.

1888[1] the blade was shortened to 37 in. and in 1892[2] the blade was again changed to that of the 1890 Cavalry pattern, $34\frac{1}{2}$ in.[3]

All the above have the same handguard except that in 1892 certain parts of the design were to be left unpierced, the guard being lined with white buckskin. This sword is in use for ceremonial at the present day, the Service sword being the Cavalry 1908 pattern.

[1] *List of Changes*, 5928.   [2] *Ibid.* 6859.

[3] A sword of the "honeysuckle" pattern (fig. 21) engraved D.3.2.R.H.G. suggests that this was worn by the Royal Horse Guards Trooper between 1829 and 1882.

CAVALRY

The generally accepted meaning of the term "Cavalry" is mounted troops who fight as such, and at any rate in the first half of the eighteenth century the use of the word "Horse" is sufficiently explanatory. At the same time it should be borne in mind that for nearly a hundred years there were certain branches of the Army which, although mounted, were primarily intended for fighting on foot, the horse being merely a means of rapid transport, the forerunner of the Mounted Infantry of yesterday and of the mechanical transport of to-day. Of this mobile infantry the chief units were the Dragoons, who appeared as Dragoniers in 1649. In a manuscript of this date entitled "A brief treatise of war",[1] it is stated that "they are to be lightly armed as may be with culverins,[2] powder flasks and swords". They are also to carry at the girdle two swyn-feathers or foot pallisados 4 ft. in length, to stick into the ground "for their defence whereas they may come to be forced to make resistance against horse". This "light" armament was, however, considerably lessened at a later date when Charles II formed a regiment of Dragoons for service in the Barbados. The warrant runs as follows:[3]

April 2, 1672

Charles R.

Our will and pleasure is that a Regiment of Dragoones which we established and ordered to be raised in Twelve Troopes of fourscore in each besides officers, who are to be under the command of Our most deare and most intirely beloved Cousin, Prince Rupert, shall be armed out of Our stoares remaining within Our Office of the Ordinance, as followeth: that is to say three corporalls, two serjeants, the gentlemen-of-armes, and twelve souldiers of each of the said troopes are to have and carry each of them one halbard and

---

[1] Brit. Mus. Harl. MSS. 6008.

[2] This is obviously "Caliver", a short matchlock musket; the culverin was a cannon of large calibre.

[3] Prince Rupert visited Barbados in 1652 and returned in 1653 but never visited the island in 1672.

one case of pistolls with holsters; and the rest of the souldiers of the severall Troopes aforesaid are to have and carry each of them one match-locke musquet with a collar of bandileers, and also to have and to carry one bayonett or greate knife. That each lieutenant have and carry one partizan and that two drums be delivered out for each troope of the said Regiment.

By His Majesty's Command

(*signed*) ARLINGTON.[1]

To SIR THOMAS CHICHELY
Master-General of the Ordnance

By this order the Dragoon officer and sergeant are apparently encumbered with long staff weapons when mounted, weapons which were of little practical use even to the dismounted man. Swords are not ordered in the warrant, but perhaps this is because they were considered to be the accepted weapon of every soldier, and therefore not worthy of mention.

In the *Military and Marine Discipline* by John Lacey, published in the same year as the warrant above quoted, 1672, it is stated that "Dragoons are but Foot on horseback" and that they are equipped with muskets (that is, carbines) 2 ft. 9 in. in length and pikes, "if allowed", not more than 13 ft. long. As both these records are of the same date, we are faced with the problem of the true meaning of the terms Partizan, Pike and Halberd. Are these all the same type of weapon but carelessly described, and how were they carried by mounted troops and how used by them on foot? The Drill or Exercise books of the period give minute instructions as to the use of sword, musket and bayonet, but none of them gives any information respecting staff weapons carried by mounted troops.

In 1687 we find that the Dragoons had muskets, bayonets and "hammer-hatchets" (? halberds) but no swords, and in 1689 they had neither muskets, bayonets nor halberds. After this date the halberd is never mentioned as part of the equipment of the Dragoon. If the Dragoon of 1672 and 1687 had no sword,

---

[1] W.O. 26/1, p. 267 and W.O. 55/333, p. 148.

he certainly needed one, for in 1691 the Colonel of the Innis-killing Dragoons wrote to the Secretary at War: "we want good cutting swords with three-bar hilts."[1] The 1st Dragoons were better off for their "return" in the same year was 480 swords and two years later the 8th Dragoons had 1180.[2] The Horse Grenadiers were also mounted for mobility, and were not expected to operate in the accepted Cavalry fashion. Their exercise and armament are briefly described on p. 37.

This unsatisfactory arrangement as regards supply became so serious that the following minute was entered in the Proceedings of the Board of Ordnance of 27 June 1796: "Great detriment having occurred at the commencement of the present War from the tardiness of supplying swords and sabres, from the excessive Badness of those manufactured in such a moment of Hurry... the Cavalry swords and sabres are in future to be issued by the Ordnance in the same manner as the firelocks and they are to undergo at the Tower a most Accurate Proof."[3] This was carried into effect on 3 May 1797 when swords were "prepared and collected at the Tower", the 15th Light Dragoons being the first regiment to receive the new issue.[4] The swords were presumably still made by outside contractors, for there was no Government factory at that date, but the order was evidently intended to insist on proof and inspection before issue. This difficulty of supply lasted for over fifty years and was only rectified after some thousands of swords had been destroyed in the great fire at the Tower of London in 1841. As by this time there were few sword-cutlers and none in a large way of business it was ordered that all Cavalry swords were to be made by the Ordnance at the public expense.[5]

OFFICERS. As far as can be gathered from contemporary prints all officers of Cavalry wore either the simple sword-hilt

[1] Col. Cliford Walton, *Standing Army*, p. 424.
[2] T. 27/14.
[3] W.O. 3/29, p. 44.   [4] W.O. 3/31, p. 39.
[5] W.O. Circular Letter, 7 March 1844.

(Plate II, 1), which was also carried by general officers and officers of Infantry regiments alike or, as they had to equip the regiment out of their own pockets, used whatever weapon took their personal fancy. The portrait of the 10th Earl of Pembroke, Colonel of the Royal Dragoons, by Reynolds, reproduced on the Frontispiece shows a carefully drawn sword-hilt of scrolled bars lined with leather, which will be referred to later. This portrait was painted in 1765 and is of value as being one of the few portraits of this period that give such a detail with accuracy. On 31 May 1788 the Board of Ordnance ordered that all officers of Cavalry regiments were to carry the same swords as the men,[1] but it is more than probable that, as they had to meet the cost, this order was often honoured rather in the breach than in the observance.

TROOPERS. The sword of the Trooper of the late seventeenth century was, more or less, based on the Cromwellian basket-hilt, from which in its turn the Highland broadsword seems to have been adapted.

We have noted before the serious shortage of weapons which is so often to be found in the eighteenth-century reports, and this is borne out by a series of letters from Colonel St Pierre of the 1st (Royal) Dragoons to Lord Raby, the Commanding Officer, which may to some extent explain the defeat which the British Army suffered at Almanza on 14 April 1707. There are frequent references to insufficient clothing, and loss of equipment and arms, and the general bad conditions which prevailed at any rate in his regiment. On 23 February 1707 he writes: "God be thanked a pretty strong Regmt. but all are naked and almost without swords." On 13 June he had evidently received some swords, of which he writes: "the swords are good but a handful too short, there is no dealing with the French but with good swords, they having excellent ones. We are all resolved if we come to Barcelona and can find German blades, to buy them and put them on our handles which are large enough." On

[1] W.O. 3/27, p. 36.

(45)

17 September he writes: "The swords sent from England are good for nothing, ours were the best....I have had the hilts which are good and strong made serve for these blades which are now pretty good and as long as any....I have got ledges of tin for the scabbards and each blade cometh to 8 shillings."[1] From the above it would seem likely that he had obtained the German blades, which he was using in preference to the English swords. There are no details as to the purpose of the tin ledges.

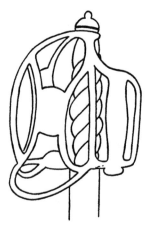 

Fig. 12. Heavy Cavalry Trooper, 1742–51. North British Fusiliers, 1751. Fig. 13. Dragoons Trooper, 1742.

In the 1742 volume referred to on p. 36 most of the Cavalry regiments carried the true Highland sword and that this must have been in use for a long period we know from a Schedule of Clothing of Killigrew's Dragoons dated 1706.[2] This schedule includes every item of equipment and mentions "Split socket-bayonets to serve over a full-bored musket", and also adds: "Basket-hilted Highland Scotch broadswords", which describes the hilt in an unmistakable manner (Fig. 12). The 1st to the 4th Horse, the 2nd Dragoon Guards and the 3rd to the 15th Dragoons are all shown with this sword, but the Royal Regiment

[1] Brit. Mus. Add. MSS. 31134, ff. 399 v, 422.
[2] A.O. 17/28, p. 154.

of Dragoons carry a sword of entirely different design and of a type which is not found in any museum or collection (Fig. 13). As the volume above mentioned shows so many Cavalry regiments with this peculiar sword, it is surprising that no examples have survived. We believe that the solution is that this hilt was carelessly drawn, the engraving being reproduced for each regiment, and that the artist endeavoured to depict a bar-hilted sword very similar to that shown on the Frontispiece and on Plate II, 15; fig. 14. There are two swords of this type in the

Fig. 14. Dragoons Officer and Trooper, 1742–65.

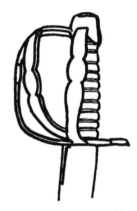

Fig. 15. Heavy Dragoon Trooper, ? 1777.

Tower, the blades 39 in. long being engraved G.R. and INCONQUERABLE. Possibly this may be the origin of the motto *Vestigia nulla retrosum* borne by the 5th Dragoon Guards who, as the 6th Regiment of Horse, wore the sword above described.

A number of cavalrymen of other regiments are illustrated facing to the right, so that it is impossible to say whether they carried either of the above patterns. Morier's drawings of 1751 show the Highland basket-hilt with variations, some having pierced designs on the guard-plate and others being plain. In the 1788 Report above referred to it is ordered that the model to be followed was the sword of the Inniskilling Dragoons: "Half basket with blade $39 \times 1\frac{5}{12}$ in." This sword was possibly the sword issued in 1777 when an inspection return on the Inniskilling Dragoons notes that "new swords are being made", but gives no hint of the pattern. These can hardly have been of Highland pattern, otherwise they would have been classed as replacements and not as "new swords", nor would the Board have taken them as a model when many Cavalry regiments were using a similar pattern. It is possible that they were brasshilted swords with straight blades (Fig. 15). Hastings-Irwin[1] considers that these had what we know as "S" hilts, but he gives no authority for his statement and it should be pointed out that careful contemporary drawings show that this peculiar sword was carried only by the Grenadier private of 1751 and possibly the Highlander of 1815.[2]

By Warrant of 14 April 1756 a Light Dragoon troop was added to each Dragoon or Dragoon Guard Regiment, just as the Light Company was added to the Line Regiment. In the same year was ordered "a short cutting sword 34 in. long with light hilt without a basket". As this sword is, with the exception of the basket, very similar to the Dragoon sword, we take leave to assume that Fig. 16, A, B, represent this weapon. Under this Warrant there were sixty privates ordered for each troop of Light Horse and at an Inspection held on 14 October of the same year their equipment is given as: swords 34 in., carbines 51 in., bayonets 17 in., and pistols, together with 63 spades, 32 handbills and 31 axes, a truly remarkable armament for a new troop specifically designated as "Light" Horse. As has been frequently pointed out in these pages the sword up to the year 1796, if not later, had to be supplied by the Colonel and it may be that for this reason the early specifications are left conveniently vague. In 1773 the 15th Light Dragoons rehilted their swords with "stirrup" hilts and this was followed by the 8th Light Dragoons who also made the same change, both keeping to the

[1] MSS. Royal United Services Institution.
[2] See pp. 73, 75.

straight blade. This "stirrup" hilt seems to be a definite improvement or variation from the simple knuckle-bow and is to

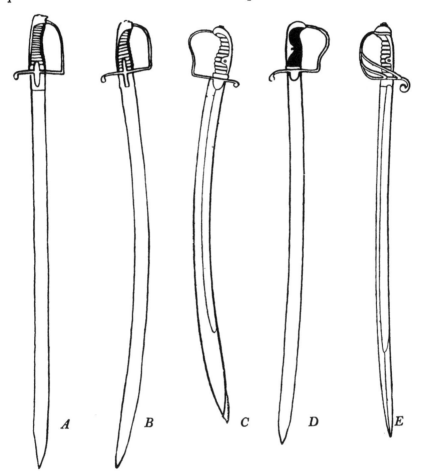

Fig. 16. Light Dragoon and Light Cavalry Trooper.
A. 1777–88. B. 1788–96. C. 1796–1820. D. 1820–29. E. 1829–53.

be found on all Light Cavalry swords of the late eighteenth and early nineteenth centuries (Fig. 16, C).

In the year 1765 the Heavy Cavalry, when dismounted, were ordered to leave their swords on their horses[1] and this practice

[1] W.O. 4/1044, p. 28.

seems to have been followed by the Light Dragoons in 1776, for the Inspecting Officer notes: "I think also that when the regiment dismounts it would be well convenient to the men to leave their swords with their horses as the dragoon regiments do." Those who have handled the Light Cavalry sword of the period will understand this, as it has a wide heavy scabbard and would be cumbersome in the extreme for the dismounted man. The above-mentioned Report of 1788 gives the measurements, blade 36 in. with a curve measuring $1\frac{3}{4}$ in. from the straight. In this Report it is added that the blades are to be tested "in a special machine" to stand a shortening of 2 in. to 1 ft. at least.[1] The Report concludes by saying that Colonels of regiments may use British or German blades "as they like".

The Napoleonic wars had brought the Hungarian Light Cavalry into prominence and their equipment and much of their uniform was copied in France and in this country. This Hungarian sword had a much more pronounced curve than the old Light Dragoon sword, for it measured in a straight line $32 \times 1\frac{1}{2}$ in. with a curve of 2 in. from the straight line. The hilt had the simple knuckle-bow and the grip was formed of two pieces of leather riveted on each side of the broad tang. This was further reinforced by two "ears" turned over on each side of the grip from the back piece (Plate III, 24; fig. 16, C).

During all this period the Light Horse had been gradually increased in numbers and several works published on their exercises and sword drill, amongst which is a work by Angelo, the noted fencing master, illustrated by Rowlandson.[2] Now the sword shown on these plates has a blade with a pronounced curve, almost of the scimitar type, and yet Angelo describes the position for the thrust, which must have been almost an impossibility. As a cutting weapon in the hands of a skilled swordsman its effect must have been terrific, indeed there is a legend that Napoleon's generals protested in the Peninsular War

[1] See p. 121.   [2] *The Hungarian and Highland Broadsword*, 1799.

against this "unsportsmanlike" behaviour of Wellington's Light Horse. As Napoleon's Light Cavalry were using the same sword we can but assume, if there is any truth in the legend, that the complaint was rather of the greater skill and more expert swordsmanship of the British cavalryman.[1] As a thrusting weapon it would be wellnigh impossible even for an expert fencer to achieve a satisfactory result.

At some date, probably in the first years of the nineteenth century, a new sword was introduced for the Heavy Cavalry, which may be termed the "disk" hilt, referred to on p. 39 (Fig. 17). On two of Hamilton-Smith's sketches in the albums preserved in the Library of the Victoria and Albert Museum this hilt is shown with full-length figures, one undated, entitled "Oxford Blues" (Royal Horse Guards), and the other 2nd Dragoons R.N.B. (Greys), dated May 1807. These are evidently drawn from life and prove that the same sword was used for Household Cavalry and for Heavy Cavalry of the Line. From the

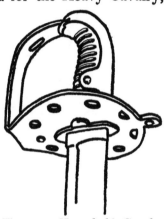

Fig. 17. Household Cavalry and Heavy Cavalry Trooper, 1807–30.

lithographs of Hull and Englemann this sword continued in use up to 1830, if not later.[2] There are several swords of this type in the Tower which have blades $34\frac{1}{4} \times 1\frac{1}{2}$ in. with hatchet-point and hence quite useless for the thrust (Plate II, 12; fig. 1, 2).

It will now simplify matters if we deal with the separate branches of the Cavalry, apart from Household Cavalry, under their respective headings, as each carried its own particular sword or swords for officers and men from 1822 up to the year 1853.

[1] Graham, *History of the 16th Light Dragoons*, I, 245.
[2] There are paintings showing these swords at Windsor in the Equerries Room, dated 1832.

HEAVY CAVALRY

OFFICERS. The *Dress Regulations* of 1822 give the sword as "guard and boat-shell" gilt (Plate II, 6) and blade 32 × 1 in., with leather scabbard and gilt mounts. For Undress the same

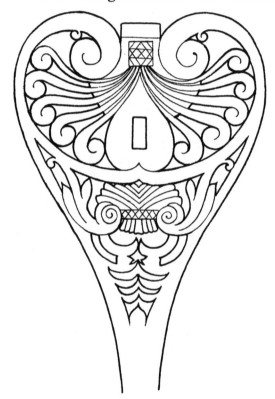

Fig. 18. Heavy Cavalry Officer, 1834.

hilt is given, but of steel, the blade 36 × 1¼ in. and the scabbard of steel.

In 1834 a new hilt was ordered, an early example of what is known as the "honeysuckle" hilt (Plate II, 16; fig. 18) with blade 35 × 1½ in. and steel scabbard. One of these swords in the Tower is ensigned W.R., which dates it between 1830 and 1837. In the 1857 *Regulations* the "honeysuckle" was abolished in favour of the "scroll" hilt of steel (Plate II, 17; fig. 19) with a $35\frac{1}{2}$ in. blade, and the same sword appears in the *Regulations* of 1874 with a new blade of 36 in. There must have been some

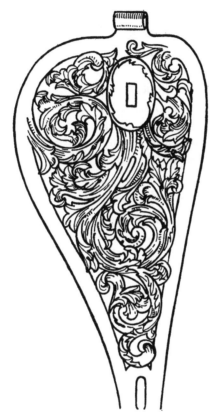

Fig. 19. "Scroll" guard, Heavy Cavalry Officer, 1857–96.
  Royal Engineers, 1857–97.
  Field Officer Black Watch, Seaforth, and Argyll and Sutherland
   Highlanders, and Highland Light Infantry.

reason of vital importance for increasing the length by $\frac{1}{2}$ in. but no details are available on this subject. In 1896 all Cavalry officers were treated alike as regards swords, which will be described further on in this chapter.

  TROOPERS. There does not appear to have been a change from the "disk" sword-hilt of 1803 till 1830 when a simple bowl-hilt was introduced lined with white buckskin (Plate II, 19; fig. 20). This was the first prac-

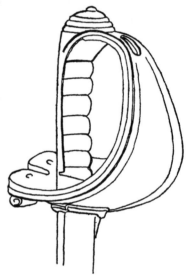

tical attempt to protect the hand, and after being altered and reduced in size it again reappears in the modern Cavalry sword.[1] The difficulties of constant supply which had exercised the War Department in 1796 became serious in 1844, up to which date swords were made by contract with outside firms, and a Circular Letter of 7 March orders that in future all Cavalry swords were to be made by the Ordnance Department. As all Cavalry were armed alike in 1853, these swords will be described later on in this chapter.

Fig. 20. Heavy Cavalry Trooper, ? 1830–53.

LIGHT CAVALRY (LIGHT DRAGOONS AND HUSSARS)

OFFICER. The *Regulations* of 1822 give a three-bar hilt (that is, a knuckle-bow and two bars outside) and a curved blade $35\frac{1}{2} \times 1\frac{1}{4}$ in. with a "pipe" back, the scabbard being of steel with a large "shoe" or drag. This sword is found in the *Dress Regulations* up to 1861, after which date the Light Dragoons disappear from the lists. In the former year the sabretache was introduced for all Cavalry.[2]

LANCERS

The Full Dress sword of Lancer officers in 1822 was the true Oriental scimitar with "Mameluke" hilt of the same type of the General Officer's sword (Plate II, 5; fig. 37) and curved blade $30 \times 1\frac{1}{4}$ in. embossed with the regimental badge. The scabbard was of crimson velvet with gilt mounts and like all Cavalry Regiments the Lancers carried the sabretache.

[1] See p. 58. [2] See p. 93.

The Service or Undress sword was the same as that of the Light Cavalry.

In 1834 the Full Dress sword was abolished, the Undress being worn on all occasions.

In 1823 the rank and file of all Light Cavalry Regiments carried the same sword. The grip, of leather and chequered, was in two parts, riveted on each side of a broad tang. The old method of piercing the grip with a narrow tang was discarded as it was considered to be weak. The guard was three-bar and the slightly curved blade 36 × 1¼ in. About 1850 there was a return to the old grip covered with fishskin bound with wire and, as formerly, the narrow tang pierced the grip. In addition the grip had a steel back, and ears on each side (Fig. 16, E). Evidently the old grip, almost circular in section, was, as one might expect, found to be unsatisfactory. It was difficult to hold firmly with a hot hand and almost impossible to use for the thrust. The steel bars of the hilt are better finished than the old pattern and the blade reduced to 35 in.

ALL CAVALRY

In 1853 the troopers, and in 1896, the officers, of all Cavalry Regiments were treated alike as to arms. The old method of having different patterns for officers and men of Heavy and Light Cavalry must have caused great difficulties as regards replacements and repairs on active service, and the amalgamation in respect of arms must have facilitated the work of the Ordnance and the Government factories.

OFFICER. By the *Regulations* of 1896 all Cavalry officers were ordered a sword with bowl-guard engraved with the "honeysuckle" pattern referred to above, with a straight blade 35⅛ in. and steel scabbard (Plate II, 18; fig. 21). This was followed on 1 March 1912 by the present Cavalry sword, which had been approved by King Edward VII on 2 July 1908.[1]

1 See p. 26.

The grip, of dermatine, is of semi-pistol shape with thumb-bowl, the whole covered with fishskin and bound with silver wire; the guard of generous bowl form is, like its predecessor of 1834, engraved with the "honeysuckle" pattern which, from changes of design and treatment, cannot at the present day be recognized as a horticultural specimen. The blade, straight, is 35 × 1 in. and the scabbard of steel had two fixed rings (Fig. 22).

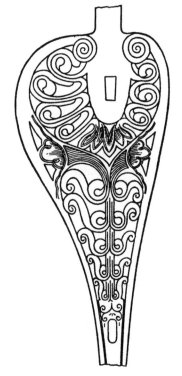 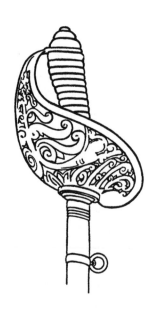

Fig. 21. Cavalry Officer, 1896.　　　　Fig. 22. Cavalry Officer, 1912.

TROOPERS. In 1853 the trooper's sword followed that of the officer of Light Cavalry, except that the grip was of two thick pieces of leather, chequered and riveted on either side of the tang, which in this case was broad, as opposed to the narrow tang which pierced the officer's grip. The guard was of the three-bar type (Plate II, 20; fig. 23) and the straight blade

$35 \times 1\frac{3}{4}$ in. with spear-point. This is described in Army Order of 9 October 1854 as "a new sword, essentially a thrusting weapon". There were obvious disadvantages in this hilt, as it was no protection to the hand except from a direct cut and even here the bars were somewhat weak.

This was remedied in 1864[1] when the sheet steel hilt known as the "Maltese Cross" hilt was introduced (Plate III, 21). The new sword must have been sent for practical testing to various Cavalry Regiments, but no one seemed to have noticed that the inner edge of the guard frayed the tunic. At a later date this edge was turned down slightly to get over the difficulty. It was at first ordered for all mounted units except the Household Cavalry, but the Royal Horse Artillery would have none of it and as a result of pressure from within it was laid down that the Artillery should continue to use the 1853 pattern.[2]

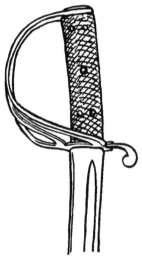

Fig. 23. Cavalry Trooper, 1853.

In 1885 the upper part of the guard was raised and then dropped towards the pommel to form a handstop and two lengths of blade issued, $35\frac{3}{8}$ and 33 in. An extraordinary entry occurs in this record, which states that the curve of the grip is to be increased "for facility in carrying at the slope".[3] There is no suggestion that this would improve the fighting qualities of the weapon and one can only regret that the record of this remarkable decision and detailed evidence for the change have not been preserved.

As compared with other European swords of this period the 1864 pattern, though by no means perfect, seems to have satisfied the authorities and no important change was made till 1890,

[1] *List of Changes*, 887. [2] *Ibid.* 2870.
[3] *Ibid.* 4854.

when an entirely new pattern was issued.[1] The same type of
grip was used but the guard was bowl-shaped, unpierced and
painted khaki for Service wear. The blade was $32\frac{1}{2} \times 1\frac{1}{4}$ in. and
the khaki painted scabbard had two fixed loops. In this weapon
the grip is too long and being rounded is difficult to hold with a
hot hand and the balance bad; at the same time it would be a
fairly good cut and thrust sword with a different grip (Plate III,
22). It was worn on the saddle and not from a belt and this
caused such inconvenience that in 1902 the 12th Lancers carried
it on the off side, a practice which was also adopted by certain
Indian Cavalry Regiments as late as 1914. Some American
regiments at one time wore the sword horizontally on the saddle
under the left leg with the hilt pointing forward. The 17th
Lancers followed the 12th in carrying the sword on the off side
and at a later date the 21st Lancers made a similar change.

In 1908 all Cavalry and Horse Artillery were ordered the
same pattern sword as that of the officers described above
(Plate III, 25).[2]

In 1900 the Indian Cavalry troopers carried the "Tulwar",
an indigenous oriental weapon with mushroom pommel, swel-
ling grip, small cross quillons and langets all of steel. The
curved blade was $30 \times 1\frac{1}{2}$ in. In 1910 this was changed to the
three-bar hilt and curved blade. The present sword of the Indian
Cavalry (pattern 1908) differs slightly from that of the British
Cavalry. The grip is of walnut wood instead of dermatine, there
is no swell on the upper part of the grip and the thumb plate,
instead of being oval, is depressed across the front of the grip and
ridged instead of chequered.

ARTILLERY

Up to the end of the sixteenth century the guns used mostly
for siege work were manned by men drawn at random from
the military forces with no separate organization. In 1716 a

---

[1] *List of Changes*, 6477.   [2] *Ibid.* 14325.

regiment was formed of two companies who were dismounted, the guns alone being horsed.

In none of the pictorial representations of troops in the eighteenth century are there any sketches or engravings of artillerymen, the *Representation of Cloathing* of 1742 and Morier's paintings of 1751 being confined entirely to Horse and Foot Regiments with no suggestion that any of these were Artillery. We can only assume therefore that the Field or Foot Artillery were armed like the Infantry and that the Horse Artillery, which was formed in 1799, were at first simply batteries of the Foot Artillery with the personnel mounted, and as such armed like the Light Cavalry. If we are right in our surmises, therefore, the officers of Foot would carry the straight shell-hilted sword and the privates the hanger of the Line Regiments.

It should be remembered that the function of the gunner was solely to work his guns and that the Fusiliers were attached to the Artillery companies for their protection. Up to the year 1754 the sergeants of Fusiliers were armed with halberds, which were abolished in this year and replaced by fusils.[1] The halberd can have had no practical value whatsoever on active service and was in all probability only used for ceremonial parades. It is possible that these halberds were lintstocks, used for holding slow match for lighting port-fires of the gunners. As these are generally found with spear-heads they may have been classed as halberds (Fig. 63). In 1770 officers[2] were ordered to parade with fusils, but whether these replaced spontoons or swords is not stated.

Hull's lithograph dated 1828 depicts a Horse Artillery officer in full dress with a cross-hilted scimitar, which is probably meant to represent the "Mameluke" hilt of the Light Cavalry, very similar to that of the General Officer's sword of 1831.

[1] Cleaveland, *Notes on the Early History of the Royal Regiment of Artillery*, p. 241. No official records have been found to bear out Cleaveland's statement.
[2] Cleaveland, *loc. cit.*

The Artillery is first mentioned in the *Dress Regulations* of 1857, wherein officers are ordered the Light Cavalry sword, and this sword with less finish was carried by sergeants and other ranks. The *Dress Regulations* of 1872 describe the scabbard of this sword as having "a large trumpet mouth and large shoe". This sword for officers, with certain varieties of blade, has persisted up to the present day (Plate III, 25).

It may be remembered that in 1876 there was an attempt to bring the Artillery into line with the Cavalry as regards swords, but as it was found that the edge of the sheet steel "Maltese Cross" hilt injured the uniform the gunners stood firm and insisted so strongly on their preference for their old weapon, known as "pattern 1853", that a regulation was issued regularizing their choice.[1]

In 1925 the N.C.O.'s and men were ordered the 1908 cavalry sword.[2]

During all this period the Field Artillery followed the mounted companies in respect of the official swords, which were of the three-bar order, and in both cases the scabbards were of steel, the Field Officers having brass scabbards. The sabretache was worn by the Artillery from 1814 to 1891. The rank and file of the Field or Foot Artillery are shown on Hamilton-Smith's plate dated 1815[3] and these wear a short sword with simple brass

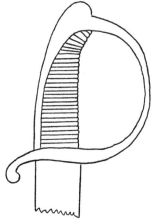

Fig. 24. Foot Artillery, 1815.

knuckle-bow hilt. There are swords of this type in the Tower Armouries, the blades dated 1830 (Fig. 24). We have no illustrations of the sergeants of this period but they probably carried the crossbar spontoon (Fig. 67), which is stated to have been in use up to 1845, fifteen years after it was abolished for

[1] *List of Changes*, 2870.   [2] *Regulations of Equipment*, Pt. 2, xi, A, 1925.
[3] *Costume of the Army of the British Empire.*

Infantry. Sergeants carried the same type of sword as the officers in 1830. The hilt was of brass and this was changed to steel in 1860. The other ranks were armed with sword-bayonets from 1853,[1] which were used with percussion and later with Snider carbines.

With the introduction of the Martini-Henri carbine of 1876 the circular ring of the hilt was "bushed", that is, reduced, to take the smaller barrel. In Bond's *Treatise of Small Arms*, dated 1884, an illustration is given of the Artillery saw-back sword-bayonet with $25\frac{3}{4}$ in. blade and 41 saw-teeth (Fig. 62). In 1897 the Field Artillery was included in "all dismounted services" as regards swords for staff-sergeants, who were allotted the same sword as the Infantry.

Fig. 25. Mountain Artillery, 1896–1902.

In 1896 a new sword was issued for Mountain Artillery chiefly in India.[2] This was a combination of the Light Cavalry sword of 1790 and the Infantry hanger of the eighteenth century. The scabbard of brown leather has brass mounts and a frog-stud (Fig. 25).

ENGINEERS

In the volumes entitled *Army Equipment*, 1865, is a short note of the previous history of this corps. In 1772 they were known as the "Soldiers Artificers Company" and this was changed in 1787 to the "Royal Military Artificers", to which title was added "Sappers and Miners" in 1812. They became the "Corps of Royal Engineers" in 1857.

There are no records of the weapons used in this corps before

[1] Lieut.-Col. H. Bond, *Treatise on Small Arms*.
[2] *List of Changes*, 8368, 9359.

the *Dress Regulations* of 1857, wherein they are ordered the "scroll" hilt of the Heavy Cavalry but brass or gun-metal instead of steel (Plate II, 17; fig. 19). The scabbard for officers was of steel and of the Field Officers brass. This sword was in use up till 1897, when the Royal Engineers followed the Infantry and all dismounted regiments with the sword shown on Plate III, 29. In 1857 the staff-sergeants were ordered the same type of hilt as that of the officers and changed, with their officers, to the 1897 pattern. The other ranks carried carbine and bayonets, the carbine of 1855 being the elliptical-bore Lancaster, the bayonets having brass mounts and fittings (Fig. 55, C). After 1871 they were armed as the rest of the army.

INFANTRY

OFFICERS. The sword of the Infantry officer as compared with that of the Cavalry officer is a simple matter. From the beginning of the eighteenth century he carried a straight-bladed weapon based on the town sword which every gentleman of means wore as part of his full dress, the military sword being, of necessity, of stouter proportions than was the case with the civilian sword, which was only used in earnest for duels and private encounters. The Infantry sword had two projecting plates at the base of the grip, known as "shells", which were survivals of the great bowl-hilt of the rapier of Elizabethan times (Plate III, 26; fig. 42). A narrow knuckle-bow completed a defence which was indeed no defence at all, but, like all men of rank at this period, the officer was expected to be expert in all forms of guard and parry, learnt in the schools of fence which abounded in England and Europe. This sword is described in an Order, dated 3 April 1786, as follows: "His Majesty orders a strong cut and thrust sword for Infantry 32 × 1 in., the hilt if not of steel to be either gilt or silver according to the buttons of the uniform."[1]

[1] H.O. 50/380.

A general order was issued, dated 18 March 1803, for a "new pattern sword" for General Officers, and officers of Grenadiers, Infantry and Light Infantry.[1]

There are several swords in the Tower of precisely the same design as that of the General Officer of 1803 which must certainly have been ordered for Guards Regiments, for the most ornate have the blades engraved GRER, GDS. WATERLOO. Others of simpler form were probably officers of flank companies. The fact that "Waterloo" appears on the blades proves that this was the type of weapon in use from 1815 to 1822, probably the latest issues before the new pattern came out (Plate II, 2; fig. 2).

In 1822 the first complete *Dress Regulations* ordered a new pattern, entirely different from any sword-hilt in this or in any European army. The guard was of gilt brass or steel fretted out in geometrical patterns reminiscent of architectural tracery. It is loosely described in the *Regulations* as "half-basket", but as this term is used for swords of varying designs we have taken the responsibility of naming this the "Gothic" hilt so that there may be no doubt as to the pattern referred to. The pommel was "stepped", the grip of fishskin

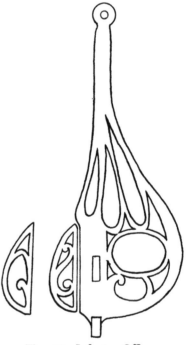

Fig. 26. Infantry Officer, handguard, 1822.

bound with gilt wire and the inner part of the guard hinged so as to fall down and fit snugly to the side. At the back of the guard was a cartouche on which were displayed the Royal Cypher and Crown. The whole guard was lined with black

[1] W.O. 3/35, p. 462.

(63)

SWORDS OF THE ARMY

patent leather and the scabbard was of black leather with gilt mounts and rings, for the new sword was worn with slings and not from a frog as was the case with the previous weapon (Plate III, 28). The blade was slightly curved, 32 in. long with a "pipe" back which is a serious drawback for cutting though it stiffens the sword for the thrust. This sword was ordered for

Fig. 27. Infantry Officer, grip and scabbard mounts, 1822.

Fig. 28. Infantry Officer, hand-guard, 1850.

all Infantry Regiments, including the Foot Guards. There are many variations of this type of handguard, as worn by generals, officers and staff-sergeants of Line Regiments and of the Departmental Corps (figs. 26–28), but they all follow the main lines as shown on fig. 28.[1]

In 1834 under the new Regulation the leather lining was

[1] There is a sword of this type in the Tower marked W.R. with a rapier blade 48 in. long. There are no records to explain the use of this weapon.

abolished for the Foot Guards and a brass scabbard introduced for Field Officers. This sword with the patent-leather lining to the guard continued in use by the Infantry officers up till 1895, but the Guards Regiments were ordered a change in the *Dress Regulations* of 1885. The gilt brass hilt was superseded by a plated steel guard of the same design, but in place of the Royal Cypher each Regiment of the Guards carries its badge upon the escutcheon. In this year also permission was given to etch, or "emboss" as it is termed, the battle honours of the Regiment on the blade. This sword is in·use at the present day, and a "light" sword of the same design is worn for levees and other ceremonies. The sword of the Rifle Regiments, of the same design but in polished steel instead of brass, the escutcheon bearing the bugle, was ordered and is still worn for ceremonial purposes.[1]

In 1895, while the Guards were left *in statu quo*, the Infantry sword was changed completely except in the case of the Highland and Rifle Regiments who continued to carry the old patterns respectively.

Pommel and grip are much the same as in the old sword but the grip is somewhat thicker. The handguard, of larger size, is of sheet steel with pierced strap-work design and bearing the Royal Cypher, the perforation being so designed that lance or bayonet will not penetrate. As a guard the hilt seems to fulfil all desiderata. The blade is $32\frac{3}{8} \times 1$ in. and the whole weapon, like its predecessor, weighs with scabbard about 2 lb. 15 oz. (Plate III, 29).

The one obvious drawback to this sword is the width of the handguard, which, like the Scottish broadsword, interferes with the free movement of the right hand and, like the Cavalry sword of 1864, the inner edge of the Infantry guard was found to chafe the tunic seriously. As a result of representations on this point in 1897 the inner edge was turned down. The scabbard is of

---

[1] Some Sergeants' swords are found with the old brass hilt and C.G. for Coldstream Guards instead of V.R.

wood covered with brown leather and has a stud to engage in
the frog on the sword-belt, a direct revival of the method of
attachment in vogue in the eighteenth century. The Royal
Cyphers which appear on early sword-blades and on the handguards of later date are given on p. 12. The controversial subject of the "Sam Browne" belt is discussed on p. 94.

The Scottish Regiments present certain difficulties as the com-
plications of "customary usage" are many and intricate. During
the last half of the eighteenth century they appear to have carried
the same sword as officers in the English Regiments (Plate III, 26)
and this was continued under the *Dress Regulations* of 1822. It
is uncertain as to when officers in Highland Regiments assumed
the national weapon and it is possible that this took place before
1830. An order of 1830 states that Highland officers are to wear
their swords on slings and not on a frog. This can hardly refer
to the swords of the Line Regiments, otherwise the Highland
Regiments would not be specifically mentioned.[1]

Under the 1831 *Regulations* the traditional Highland broadsword, still erroneously called the "claymore", similar to that
shown on Plate III, 32 was regularized. It should be pointed out
that the true "claymore" or Claidheamh-mor was a two-handed
sword with plain quillons sloped towards the blade. The present
pattern, developed from the Schiavona of the Venetians, had,
under different names and with differences in detail, been in use
since the early part of the seventeenth century, not only in the
Highlands but also in the hands of Cromwell's troopers. It is a
matter of some interest to note that this weapon must have been
in favour with the Cavalry in the early seventeenth century, as
witness the Schedule of Equipment for the Dragoons of 3 March
1707[2] in which "Basket-hilted Highland Scotch broadswords"
are mentioned with a note that out of 306 on paper 206 are
"wanting". The 1834 *Regulations* order the guard to be lined
with white buckskin edged with blue silk ribbon and covered on
the outside with scarlet cloth, the pommel having a silk tassel.

[1] W.O. 3/428, p. 204. [2] A.O. 17/28, p. 154.

The blade, straight, $32 \times 1\frac{1}{2}$ in., was two-edged and therefore a true "cut and thrust" weapon. The guard constricts the hand considerably in rapid sword play but it should be remembered

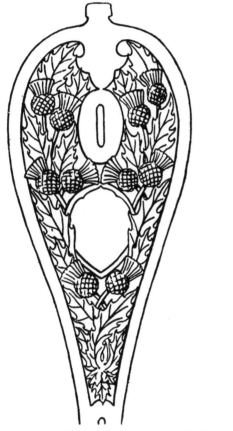

Fig. 29. "Thistle" handguard, Field Officer Royal Scots, Gordon Highlanders, King's Own Scottish Borderers, Royal Scots Fusiliers.

Fig. 30. Grip for "Thistle" guard.

that originally it was used purely for cutting, the guarding being effected by the leather targe or the dirk carried in the left hand. In 1863 an improved pattern was introduced, and this with minor alterations is in use at the present day. In addition to the basket-hilt, a plain cross-hilt which could be interchanged by

SWORDS OF THE ARMY

unscrewing the pommel was introduced in 1883 for the Highland
Light Infantry, but it is only ordered "for levees, etc." In this
year the Cameronians (Scottish Rifles) were ordered to carry
the same sword as the Rifle Regiments. The *Regulations* from
1894 onwards make no change as regards the Highland Regiments but specify that the basket-hilt was to be used only for
levees, etc., and the cross-bar for "other occasions", by the
Scottish Regiments "Wearing Trews", that is, the Royal Scots,
the King's Own Scottish Borderers and the Royal Scots Fusiliers.
None of these regulations mentions any swords for mounted
officers, but during the last twenty years the following have been
adopted as "customary". The swords of all mounted officers in
Scottish Regiments with one exception are interchangeable with
the "claymore" hilt. On Figs. 29, 30 will be found the "thistle"
hilt and grip used by the Gordons, the Royal Scots, the King's
Own Scottish Borderers and the Royal Scots Fusiliers, the blank
space being filled with the regimental badge. The Field Officers
of the Black Watch, the Highland Light Infantry, the Seaforth
and the Argyll and Sutherland Highlanders use the Heavy
Cavalry sword-hilt, with "scroll" (pattern 1857–96) as shown on
Fig. 19. All these hilts are lined, like the "claymore", with
white buckskin and scarlet cloth.

The Queen's Own Cameron Highlanders have adopted an
entirely different hilt for Field Officers. The hilt, which is fixed
and not removable, is the three-bar hilt of the Royal Artillery
with a Cavalry blade, pattern 1896 (Fig. 31).

About the year 1878, when the sword was still a weapon of
offence, it was realized that the basket-hilt was most inconvenient and it was ordered that for active service it should be
replaced by the cross-hilt which, as regards its protection,
was far worse; for, be it remembered, the knight of the four-
teenth century who was armed with such a weapon had a shield
in his left hand and a gauntlet of mail or plate on his right hand.

The use of the cross-bar led to more "customary" changes,
which will be found noted in detail on Fig. 32.

(68)

Finally, we have the *Dress Regulations* of 1934, which order that, except for Cavalry, swords are not to be worn in marching order or on service. It is also laid down that swords are not to be worn at mess or stables, but in the case of the Worcestershire Regiment the Orderly Officer or Captain of the week may wear the sword with mess dress. The traditional reason for this single exception is that when encamped on St John's Island, now Prince Edward Island, in 1746, the Worcesters were surprised at mess and their arms, which were in another tent, were captured. Whatever the true story, the Worcestershire Regiment still bears the soubriquet "The Ever-sworded".

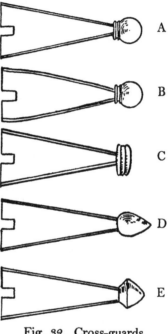

Fig. 31. Handguard, Field Officer Cameron Highlanders

Fig. 32. Cross-guards.

A. Seaforth, Cameron and Argyll and Sutherland Highlanders.

B. Highland Light Infantry and Royal Scots Fusiliers.

C. Royal Scots.

D. Black Watch and Gordon Highlanders.

E. King's Own Scottish Borderers.

SERGEANTS. The title of Sergeant is of ancient origin, dating at least from the thirteenth century, but it is only in the eighteenth century that we find the name specifically applied to the highest rank of non-commissioned officer. Like all soldiers mounted or dismounted he carried a sword and in addition he carried a halberd (Fig. 65). In Captain Sime's *Military Guide*, 1778, it is laid down that all sergeants are to carry swords but no mention is made of the halberd. In the list of equipment of the 16th Foot (1757) the sergeants' swords are brass-hilted and in the same year those of the 29th Foot silver-mounted.[1] In 1791 it was ordered that the fusil or short musket was to be substituted for the halberd in the case of sergeants of Grenadiers. There are few contemporary drawings of sergeants, but from the fact that there still exist a number of swords of the same pattern as those of the officers but of inferior finish we can only assume that these were the sergeants' weapons.

The spontoon, or sergeant's pike (Fig. 67), introduced about 1799, displaced the halberd in all Infantry Regiments and was abolished in 1830. It will be dealt with in detail on p. 116. It has been noted above that the sergeant's sword followed the pattern of the officer's sword, and although there is no written evidence on the subject the examples in the Tower prove that the same procedure was followed when the new officer's sword was introduced in 1822 (Plate III, 28). Some of these have cast brass grips, possibly adapted from earlier Grenadier and other swords. In all the inventories these swords are classed as staff-sergeants' swords, or in brief "S.S." The staff-sergeant does not exist to-day as a title but the term applies to battalion, as distinct from company sergeants. It also applies to sergeants of Departmental Corps such as Ordnance, Medical, Army Services, etc. It would be wearisome to recapitulate the changes of weight, length and other details of staff-sergeants' swords throughout the *List of Changes* from 1860 to 1895 comprising over a dozen entries. In 1888 we find a definite and more useful entry,[2] in which it is laid down that the brass hilt is allotted to staff-sergeants of dismounted Royal Engineers, Infantry—except Highland and Rifle Regiments—and Medical Staff Corps;

[1] T. 14/13, pp. 233, 279, 308.   [2] *List of Changes*, 5627.

the steel hilt being ordered for dismounted Royal Artillery and all other Departmental Corps.

When the officer's sword was changed in 1895 the staff-sergeant's followed suit two years later for all dismounted troops, including Guards regiments, except Highland regiments and Highland volunteers.[1] Before the year 1828 the Scottish sergeant seems to have carried a broadsword with bronze or brass hilt, for a Circular Letter in the War Office Library dated 12 September 1828 lays down that the Highland sword should have a steel hilt, and the same material has been employed up to the present day.

PRIVATES. The sword of the private was always, from the days of Cromwell's pikemen, a "last resort" weapon. In those times, when his 15-ft. pike was broken, he had only a sword to rely upon, and the same may be said of his comrade with the cumbersome matchlock musket. In 1702 the pike was abolished for regiments of foot and the musket and bayonet were brought into use.[2] The foot soldier was now encumbered with musket, bayonet and sword, to say nothing of his capacious pouch and priming horn, the sword being still intended for close-quarters fighting. Apparently the English foot soldier disliked the weapon, for Gaya writes under "Les Troupes Angloises": "Les Fantassins ne se servent presque pas d'Epées et quand ils ont fait la décharge du Mousquet ils se battent a coups de Croise",[3] a primitive form of attack which has given rise to the saying "give them the butt". Still, the sword was there and in a complicated variety of design. In the *Representation of Cloathing* of 1742, to which we have so often referred, the sword of the Infantry had a simple shell-hilt and knuckle-bow, usually called a "hanger" (Figs. 33–36; Plate III, 30), but there are so many varieties of this weapon in the Tower and elsewhere that we must assume that the Colonels of each regiment, who had to pay for the arms, favoured different designs. In the Store Vouchers

---

[1] *List of Changes*, 8823.   [2] W.O. 26/11, p. 272 (187).
[3] *Traité des Armes*, p. 157.

of 1701–2, a period when the whole of Europe was in arms over the Spanish Succession, large numbers of Infantry swords were received into and issued from the Tower. One entry alone gives 5000, and a perusal of this volume will show that the number was greatly increased throughout Marlborough's campaigns.[1] Again, in 1743–4 there are more issues, including 1000 "Land Service swords", among which are 100 described as "Dog-headed".[2]

When we come to the Grenadier companies we are overwhelmed with a spate of sword-hilts many of which can only be guessed at. One Grenadier sword of the 23rd Welch Fusiliers in the 1742 record has a somewhat flimsy hilt (Plate III, 31), the same type being found in Morier's drawing of a Grenadier of the 31st Regiment in 1751. From Morier's drawings, referred to on p. 10, which deal only with Grenadiers, the varieties of hilt can only be dealt with by conjecture, for they include Scottish basket-hilts, knuckle-bows and other designs which, from the position in the drawing, cannot be identified from existing examples (Fig. 12). The mere fact that there were so many designs in use explains the continual shortage in Inspections and Returns, for the Colonel had no store from which to draw regulation swords, but had to replace the weapons of his choice, not infrequently from Germany.

As the officer, like the citizen of rank, carried his sword when "walking out" the private followed suit, with the result that tavern and street brawls were frequent. In 1763 it was ordered that all Regiments of Foot in Great Britain, Gibraltar and Minorca shall do duty without swords;[3] and again we find the Governor of St Helena writing to the Governors of the East India Company in 1767:[4] "We think it may not be very proper for your private soldiers to wear swords in such a drinking place as St Helena is, except when they are on duty." In the long

---

[1] W.O. 49/222 *passim*.
[2] W.O. 49/238.
[3] W.O. 4/73, p. 235.
[4] Colonel Clifford Walton, *Standing British Army*, 1894, p. 439.

Fig. 33. Infantry "Hanger",
1742.

Fig. 34. Infantry "Hanger",
1751.

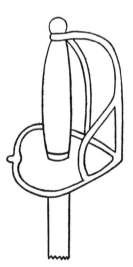

Fig. 35. Infantry Private, 35th Foot,
1751.

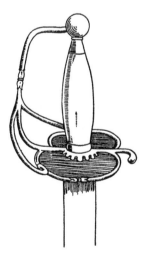

Fig. 36. Infantry Private,
1751.

series of volumes of Inspections in the Public Record Office[1] the following reports are to be found under their respective dates. In 1745 the swords of the 33rd Regiment, reported as "very bad", were left in store at Ghent and captured by the French. Swords were evidently lost or damaged, for under the dates 1756 and 1758 we find new swords provided for the 52nd and 53rd Regiments respectively. In 1768 the 25th Regiment was inspected and it was reported that they had no swords. This constant deficiency of weapons was, to a large extent, due to the fact that much of the private's equipment had to be met from "off-reckonings". The system was, briefly, that the Government paid the Colonel a sum based on the strength, that is, the "paper" strength, of the regiment. Of this sum a certain portion was ear-marked as "subsistence money" and out of the residue there was a sum, which was called "nett off-reckonings", from which clothing, swords and other necessaries were purchased. It is therefore easily understood that a Colonel who had little pride in the turn-out of his regiment would save money on swords, more especially if there were no definite orders for their provision. As the price in the middle of the eighteenth century was 5s. 2d. for an infantry "hanger", presumably without the scabbard, which cost one shilling,[2] it will be seen that the provision of swords for a regiment at full strength was a financial consideration.

At last this unsatisfactory condition of affairs impressed upon the military authorities the need for drastic action, and in 1768[3] a Royal Warrant was issued in which it was ordered that: "All Sergeants and the whole Grenadier Company are to have swords, the corporals and men of the Battalion companies, except the Regiment of Royal Highlanders, to have no swords." Here it is emphasized that the Royal Highlanders, the 42nd

[1] W.O. 27/1–60.
[2] Colonel Mackinnon, *Origin and Services of the Coldstream Guards*, 1833, II, 338, 359.
[3] W.O. 30/13 B, p. 16.

Regiment, are still to carry swords. But Highlanders have ever been a law unto themselves and in 1775 they decided that though decorative for dress and ceremonial they preferred the bayonet, a preference which was probably founded on the fact that the Highland broadsword is not a convenient weapon to handle, especially if used in conjunction with the musket. A peremptory order was issued that the regulations were to be observed, but we have no records of the immediate results. Eight years after they settled the matter in Nova Scotia by returning all their swords to the Ordnance Store at Halifax. Evidently other regiments followed the lead of their Scottish comrades, and in the following year an order dated 21 July 1784 was issued abolishing the sword for infantrymen.[1] Still the Highlander had his own views as to carrying out regulations, and Highland swords are noted as part of the equipment of 1798.

There are so many varieties of the Highland broadsword-hilt in the eighteenth century that it is quite impossible to illustrate them. Indeed, these are as often as not personal and not regimental weapons. Most of them have blades signed by the mysterious Andrea Ferrara, whose swords must have been imported, as we have no evidence that he ever worked in Scotland. The prints by Sebastian Müller in the British Museum must be dated not later than 1789 when Müller ceased working, and these show the Infantry wearing typical Highland swords. Another print in the same collection by Saint Fal, published in 1815, during the occupation of Paris by the Allies, shows a Highlander, presumably a sergeant, with a very carefully drawn "S"-hilted sword (Plate III, 31) which can hardly have been depicted if the artist had not seen it.

In the year 1784 the 22nd Regiment adopted the tomahawk in emulation of their enemies the North American Indians (Fig. 69). This, with the Musket, Rifle and Bayonet, will be dealt with later.

[1] W.O. 4/73, p. 235.

PIONEERS

The early Pioneer was, obviously, the agricultural labourer pressed for service with the Army, but, as time went on and military operations were more extended, it was necessary to have men serving in the Army for road-making, tree-felling, making earthworks and such like duties. With the advent of artillery, the earliest patterns of which were, for the most part, heavy and of large calibre, the Pioneer was attached to the gunners, for, as numerous entries in the State Papers bear witness, much heavy work had to be done in road-making and preparing positions before the battery could come into action.

In a Royal Warrant of 28 May 1689 Pioneers are scheduled as carrying an axe and "hanger", the latter being the sword of the foot soldier described on p. 71. In a warrant of 1768 they were equipped with axe, saw and apron, but no mention is made of the sword. Nine years later a return of the 32nd Foot dated 23 January 1777 gives Pioneer caps, leather aprons, axes and saws with cases and slings for the same.

In the middle of the nineteenth century the saw-back sword was introduced; very efficient as a saw but producing terrible wounds when used as a sword.

During the War of 1914–18 the Press and the whole of the uninformed civilian world were horrified at the report that the German army was using this "diabolical weapon", oblivious to the fact that every army in Europe had used a precisely similar sword and in this country an exact counterpart to the German sword had been part of the Pioneer's equipment for nearly fifty years. In the early part of the nineteenth century the Pioneer was evidently armed with a musket in addition to his other impedimenta, for in 1856 the musket was withdrawn and a saw-backed sword issued[1] (Plate III, 33) which was withdrawn in 1903.[2] In this *List of Changes* Pioneer swords are scheduled as obsolete and for "Naval Service" with a reference to an Admiralty Letter

[1] W.O. General Order 18 November 1856.   [2] *List of Changes*, 12058.

which unfortunately, with other papers on obsolete arms, has been destroyed as of no further interest. It is therefore impossible to say why these very peculiar weapons were dealt with by the Admiralty. The Pioneer of the nineteenth century was a picturesque figure, even up to our own time. He was, by official order, bearded, wore a large pipe-clayed apron and carried a great woodman's axe (Fig. 70). At the end of the century there were ten Pioneers to each battalion, but these no longer wielded axe or saw-back sword for they comprised three carpenters, two masons, one farrier, one stone-mason, one glazier and two plumbers.[1]

BAND

All through the eighteenth century and indeed up to about the year 1824, the Regimental Band, or "Music" as it was styled, was a purely private organization paid for and equipped by the Colonel and his officers. According to Everard[2] the men were not attested, that is to say, they did not form part of the Regiment as servants of the Crown till after 1824 when they were enlisted as soldiers.[3]

In 1770 the Royal Dragoons seem to have employed boys as "Music" and returned them as "rank and file" in order to increase the paper strength of the Regiment. This was discovered and the Colonel was ordered to replace them by "effective Dragoons".[4] There was no authorized enlisting of bandsmen at the beginning of the nineteenth century, but this was sometimes done *sub rosa*. In one instance in 1824 it was discovered that the Sergeant-Master of the Band had been so enlisted with the result that the Horse Guards state that "His Royal Highness declines to sanction any deviation from the Regulations and Usage of the Army".[5]

[1] *The British Army*, by "A Lieutenant-Colonel", 1899.
[2] *History of Thomas Farrington's Regiment.*
[3] W.O. 3/405, p. 234.
[4] W.O. 3/25.   [5] W.O. 3/405, p. 234.

The Drums, Fifes and, in the Cavalry, the Trumpeters were not part of the "Music", but were an integral part of the fighting forces, being employed from the sixteenth century onwards in sounding retreats, charges, and other calls or signals. Everard states that in 1785 twelve men were enlisted in Hanover for the Coldstream Guards and of these three were negroes. The employment of coloured musicians was common at this period, the last of these being in the Band of the 29th Foot in 1843, after which they disappear.

The only weapons of the Band were swords and, as they were provided from the Colonel's private purse, these were of different designs as choice or expense dictated. In 1781 the Royal Warrant laid down that the Drums and Fifes should carry a "short sword with 'scimitar' blade"[1], but no indication is given of the design of the hilt. This is possibly the ordinary Infantry sword shown on Fig. 33, but at the same time it is somewhat remarkable that the Warrant does not simply order the sword as worn by the Infantry. In the engraving of the "March of the Guards to Finchley" by Hogarth, dated 1750, the fifer's sword is not very clearly shown. It may be the ordinary private's "hanger", but there are some indication of bars similar to those on the "old drummer's sword" mentioned in *Army Equipment*, 1866, as used by the Hospital Corps (Fig. 40). The fact that a "scimitar" blade is specified suggests that it may have been nearer the true Oriental scimitar than the Infantry sword, which had a less pronounced curve.

In an inspection in 1770[2] the drummers of the 22nd Foot had no swords, and in 1772 those of the 30th Foot had non-regulation swords. There are few representations of bandsmen in the eighteenth century and where they occur the sword-hilt is discretely hidden from view. In the lithographs by Hull and Englemann, frequently referred to in these pages, the Band and Buglemen of 1829 are shown with a brass-hilted sword with lion-head pommel, from which we can date the many varieties which are still preserved in the Tower. These have for the most part a curved "scimitar" blade and "Mameluke" hilt, an Oriental fashion which overspread Europe in the Napoleonic period and extended to Hussars, Lancers and ultimately to General Officers. Many regiments used a special type of hilt which embodied the regimental crest or badge. Cavalry used a sword with a horse-head for pommel, Guards a lion-head, and Scottish emblems and devices abound. This practice was followed by the Militia, as is testified by the large number of these

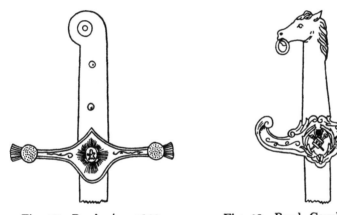

Fig. 37. Band, *circa* 1820.   Fig. 38. Band, Cavalry, *circa* 1820.

swords in the Tower marked "Oxford Militia" (Figs. 37, 38; Plate III, 35).

There are no early records extant of the introduction of the sealed pattern sword for all Infantry bandsmen except for Highland Regiments. The Infantry pattern Mark I was probably issued about 1857 when so many changes were made, the earliest patterns being marked V.R. These swords were ordered for all bands, but in the official specifications the musicians are still ignored and two types only are given, Drummer's and Bugler's, the first-named being brass- and the second steel-hilted (Plate III, 36). This hilt, like the officer's and sergeant's swords of the period, was based upon architectural motifs, the drummer's sword with small knob on the pommel, the bugler's pommel being left plain. The blade was straight, 19 in. long. Either there was a shortage of blades in the change over or some Commanding Officers were as conservative as they dared be, for there are swords in the Tower and elsewhere which have the new regulation hilt with the old long scimitar blade.

In 1895 a simpler hilt was substituted, known as Mark II (Plate III, 37), and it was ordered that all previous patterns were to be used up and declared obsolete.[1] In the *List of Changes* of 1901 (No. 9019) is an order that all swords, including drummers', must be sharpened "before going on service". This was towards the end of the South African War. When we take into consideration the long-range fighting in this campaign it seems to be remarkable that there should be any indication that drummers might be involved in hand-to-hand fighting, but this is a matter for the military historian and does not affect the design of the sword. In the beginning of each recent reign there are orders for the Royal Cypher to be altered to E.R. and G.R.V. respectively. In 1903[2] the buglers' swords were declared obsolete, the brass-hilted sword serving only for the Bands of Guards Regiments. The dirk carried by Highland drummers and pipers is of the usual national type. In 1871 the grip of the Mark I pattern was marked "HIGHLANDERS" which is omitted from the Mark II of 1902.[3] The blade is engraved with thistles. There are no regulations for Cavalry Bands, nor are there any orders abolishing non-regulation patterns. The only distinct specification is that for the Household Cavalry mentioned on p. 41 wherein a short sword is ordered for the Band with the same hilt as that of the trooper.

[1] *List of Changes*, 7953.
[2] *Ibid.* 12058.
[3] *Ibid.* 3504, 11290.

THE DEPARTMENTAL CORPS

ROYAL ARMY SERVICE CORPS. In the seventeenth century the Waggon or Transport train consisted of civilian carters controlled by "Commissaries" who were generally Staff Officers, and there does not appear to have been any purely military organization till 1794 when the "Corps of Royal Waggoners" was formed. There are no records extant of the weapons, if any, of this Corps. Presumably they were so far behind the line that their defence consisted of an escort of Cavalry or Infantry as the case might be. The officer's sword of the Waggon Train given in the *Dress Regulations* of 1831 is that of the Light Dragoons, a three-bar hilt with curved pipe-back blade.

The Waggon Train was disbanded in 1833 and was hastily reorganized as the Land Transport Corps in 1855 for the Crimea (Fig. 39; Plate III, 34). We have no information as to the officers' swords, but we have preserved in the Tower a large number of the swords of the other ranks. These are broad-bladed, short swords with brass cross-hilts based on the French Infantry sword of the period. The Corps was disbanded in 1857, but the officers reappear in the *Regulations* of the same year still carrying the Light Cavalry sword.

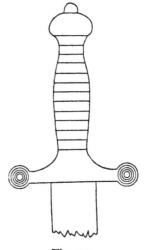

Fig. 39.
Land Transport Corps,
1855–7.

In the volumes of *Army Equipment* (1865) the Commissariat Staff has the same sword as the Infantry (Plate III, 28; figs. 27, 28), and the Military Train continues to use the Light Cavalry sword. It is further noted that "Carbines are carried on carriages and not by the men" and that swords are carried by staff-sergeants, sergeants, trumpeters and artizans. In 1875 the Commissariat and Transport were combined into one Corps and the

Dress Regulations of 1883 give them the Infantry sword of the period, the hilt lined with black leather and a brass scabbard.

In 1888 the Army Service Corps was constituted by Royal Warrant and by the *Dress Regulations* of 1891 the officers carried the same swords as those worn by Artillery officers.

ROYAL ARMY MEDICAL CORPS. There was no definite organization of medical services till the Crimea, but there were certainly medical officers as early as 1831, for in the *Dress Regulations* of that date the Medical Corps are ordered the same sword as the Infantry and this is repeated year by year till 1883. In the *Army Equipment* of 1865 it is laid down that sergeants of the Medical Staff Corps are to carry sword-bayonets instead of the "obsolete drummer's sword" which they had probably carried in the Crimea (Fig. 40). The bayonet is given as for Snider or Lancaster carbines "non-inter-changeable". In 1888 it is laid down that the hilt of the staff-sergeants' sword of the Medical Corps is "gilding metal".[1] It would appear that the old drummers' swords mentioned above must have been in use after they had been discarded in 1865, for it is not until the *List of Changes* 1888 that this sword is declared obsolete.[2]

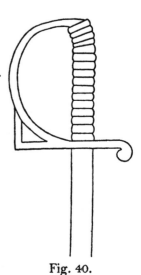

Fig. 40.

Army Hospital Corps, 1865.

ARMY ORDNANCE CORPS. The early history of this Corps is so involved, linked with Artillery and Engineers, that it is impossible to disentangle the duties now carried on solely by the Ordnance.

At first the term Ordnance was used for artillery, then it included stores of weapons and munitions as distinct from Commissariat and eventually in 1825 it became the "Store Branch", expanded to "Military Store Branch" in 1857; and in 1881,

[1] *List of Changes*, 5629.   [2] *Ibid.* 5627.

when the Army Service Corps was separated from the Store Branch, the "Ordnance Store Corps" was formed. Three years later the *Dress Regulations* order for this Corps the Infantry officer's sword with brass scabbard, the sword-hilt being of gilt brass with leather lining. The staff-sergeant's sword of 1888 was the same as the officer's but with steel scabbard.[1]

ARMY PAY DEPARTMENT. The swords of this branch of the Army are the same as those of the Ordnance. The Department was formed in 1875 and the title first appears in the *Dress Regulations* of 1883. Both the Ordnance and Army Pay Department now follow the Infantry.

ARMY VETERINARY DEPARTMENT. From the early years of the eighteenth century each Cavalry Regiment had its farriers who practised rough-and-ready surgery on the horses, but as the supply of horses was constant very little trouble was taken to patch up an invalid for future service. In 1792 a Veterinary College was started in Camden Town and in 1796 a qualified surgeon from the college was attached to each regiment of Cavalry. This arrangement lasted till 1881, when the present department was organized for purely military purposes with a college of its own. The Veterinary officers are first mentioned in *Dress Regulations* under the date 1861 and the sword allotted to them was that of the Light Dragoons. From that date up to the present day they have carried the Cavalry sword.

ROYAL NAVY

At the beginning of the nineteenth century Naval officers wore what swords they pleased, generally the straight shell-hilted sword worn by most officers in the Army. In 1805 the Board of Admiralty conjointly with Lord Nelson ordered sealed pattern swords to be deposited at Portsmouth and Plymouth but no record remains of the design of these swords.[2]

[1] *List of Changes*, 5629.
[2] Parliamentary Paper, 1842, vol. XXVII, 343.

On 1 January 1825 the Board were more explicit and illustrated their *Uniform Regulations* with lithographic illustrations.

The commissioned officer's sword was a straight 32-in. blade with ivory grip, lion-head pommel, simple knuckle-bow and langets engraved with anchor and cable, the scabbard of black leather with gilt mounts (Fig. 41). The masters, gunners, etc., had the same sword with black grip and no lion-head pommel; the physician and secretary retained the Court sword with shells, the grip having a plate engraved with the anchor (Fig. 42). The midshipman was ordered the same sword but in consideration of his stature "of such a length as may be convenient".

In 1827 the Navy followed the Army, or might it not be more discreet to say that the reverse was the case. Whichever is the truth, the Navy adopted the "Gothic" hilt, but the tracery of the Naval sword is not pierced as is the case with the Army weapon. The escutcheon bears the crowned anchor. The lion-head pommel and white grip are retained (Fig. 43). The midshipman's dirk has the same grip and pommel, but with cross-guard only. The swords of warrant officers have no lion-head and the grips are of black leather.

In 1842 we find that "Officers are at liberty to wear Dress swords", and as a result some Admirals adopted the "Mameluke" hilt of the Generals in the Army with crowned anchor on the langets instead of badges of rank. The actual pattern for this hilt is preserved by the Wilkinson Sword Company, and colour plates of uniform purveyors of the period show this sword (Fig. 44).

Evidently the "Naval Field-Marshal" was a novelty at that time, for a spirited caricature in the Windsor Library shows a mounted Admiral at full gallop with the new sword flying at his back.

All these swords are in use at the present day except the "Mameluke", which only lasted for ten years at most.

The Naval cutlass was and is still a simple weapon, more adapted for cut than thrust. The handguard of sheet steel had at

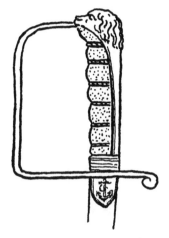

Fig. 41. Naval Flag Officer,
1825.

Fig. 42. Naval Secretary and
Physician, 1825.

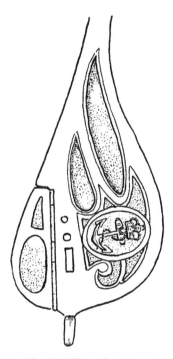

Fig. 43. Naval Officer, handguard, 1827.

first a scalloped edge (Fig. 45). In 1828 a new pattern was ordered in which the handguard was of plain steel very similar to that of the Heavy Cavalry of 1840. In 1841 a new pattern with special "grip handles" was introduced and all the old patterns were sent to the Tower for alteration, but were destroyed in the great fire at the storehouse in October of the same year.[1] In 1845 there was an endeavour to make good this loss by converting 10,000 Cavalry swords to Naval cutlasses and in 1848

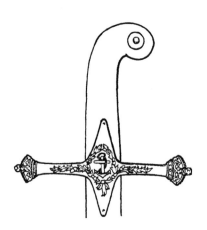
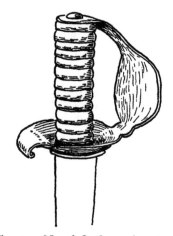

Fig. 44. Admiral, 1842–56.   Fig. 45. Naval Cutlass, *circa* 1800.

35,524 blades were ordered from Mole, Harvey and Heighington at 5s. each. In 1860 the blades were $25\frac{1}{2}$ in. and these were changed to 27 and 29 in. in 1875. In 1887 another alteration was made and the 29-in. blades were shortened to 27 in.[2] In all these swords, which were supplied by the Board of Ordnance, the handguards were blacked. The grips, at first of moulded cast-iron, were in 1900 of two-piece leather riveted on to the tang like the Cavalry sword of 1853. In 1889 the guard was of bright steel, the inner edge turned down to prevent chafing the clothing, and the blade altered again to 28 in.[3] (Figs. 46, 47).

[1] Parliamentary Paper, 1842, vol. xxvii, 343.
[2] *List of Changes*, 2808, 5353.   [3] *Ibid.* 5848.

Under an Admiralty order of 22 October 1936 (No. 4572) it is laid down that "the cutlass is no longer to form part of the equipment of men landed for service" and is merely retained for ceremonial parades. A few cutlasses are kept in each ship for this purpose regulated according to the ship's complement.

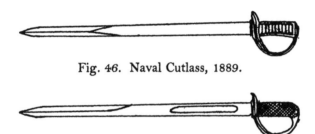

Fig. 46. Naval Cutlass, 1889.

Fig. 47. Naval Cutlass, 1900.

The Naval sword-bayonet is referred to on p. 110. According to Command Paper 5115 (1887), in the year 1859, 30,000 of these were made at Liége and 48,000 at Birmingham to fit the Snider rifle; these were adapted in 1871 for the Martini-Henry. The Boarding-Pike and Boarding-Axe are dealt with on pp. 118, 119.

Belts, Slings, Knots, etc.

BELTS, SLINGS, KNOTS, ETC.

SWORD-BELTS

The sword-belt of the sixteenth century, particularly that used for the rapier, had a hanger of loops or hooks to which the scabbard was attached, and towards the end of the century the Cavalry and Infantry sword was carried in a "frog", the scabbard having a hook which engaged in a slit in the frog. There are many references to belts in the several War Office and other papers which will be most conveniently dealt with under their respective dates:

1692. 6 July. The 6th Dragoons had gold-fringed belts for Captains and silver-fringed belts for Lieutenants and Cornets.

1713. 22 April. The Queen's Own Regiment of Dragoons, privates, have shoulder-belts laid over with broad gold lace.[1]

1727. 30 October. "His Majesty has signified his pleasure that all Horse do wear cross-belts of plain buff instead of those ornaments of lace which several now have."[2]

1729. 20 November. Buff or buff-coloured accoutrements ordered, viz. shoulder-belt with pouch, a waist-belt sufficient to carry the sword with place to receive the bayonet.[3]

1736. 20 May. Ordered new cross-belts of the best buff that can be had in England "for every tenth clothing". The cross-belt of the Dragoons in the *Representation of Cloathing* of 1742 shows a blue flask-string.

1751. The 42nd Highlanders have shoulder-belts for their broadswords.

1754. 25 October. In an inspection of the Scots Greys it is noted that the buff accoutrements are coloured white.

1756. Warrant of 14 April orders for the new Light Dragoons tanned-leather shoulder-belt $3\frac{1}{4}$ in. broad with leather cartouch-box.

[1] *Daily Courant*, sub anno. [2] W.O. 71/6, p. 134.
[3] W.O. 71/6, p. 132.

1759. 5 June. In the orderly books of the Scots Greys it is noted that shoulder-belts and slings are to be whitened and dirty waist-belts cleaned.

1765. The Frontispiece of the present volume shows Lord Pembroke's waist-belt of white leather with two gold stripes with blue stripe between, in the centre two stripes of gold with red stripe between, gilt runner and steel chain to scabbard, the sword-hilt lined buff leather.

1768. Warrant of 19 December orders officers of the Scots Greys plain white sword-belt with gilt buckle, worn round the waist. Privates to have white shoulder belts $4\frac{1}{2}$ in. wide with yellow metal buckles and waist-belts $2\frac{3}{4}$ in. wide.

1776. The 4th Horse (Dragoon Guards) have black and gold sword-knots.[1]

1787. 30 November. Heavy Cavalry are ordered to wear their swords slung over their coats. By a General Order of 8 December officers are ordered when on duty with sashes to have their swords over their uniforms, and when without sashes to wear them over their waist-belts.

1788. 3 January. Up to this period one epaulette only was worn on the left shoulder. By the new order an epaulette is to be worn also on the right shoulder to hold the sword-belt.[2]

1795. For reviews the 2nd Dragoon Guards are to have a blue strap edged with red on the right shoulder to contain the sword-belt.[3]

1796. 7 November. New pattern for Heavy Cavalry officers approved, consisting of belt and sword-knot and black leather pouch to hold 12 cartridges and shoulder-belt for the same.[4]

1796. 14 November. Sword-belts of all Cavalry to be buff colour for Regiments with that facing, white for others. Some few Regiments of Light Dragoons have supplied themselves

[1] T. 14/15, p. 391. [2] W.O. 3/7, p. 1.
[3] Standing Orders of the Queen's Dragoon Guards, 1745, p. 42. Brit. Mus. 288. e. 22 (i).
[4] W.O. 3/29, p. 131.

with red morocco belts, they can wear them till they are worn out and then conform to orders.[1]

On 22 June of this year it was ordered that the sword for Heavy Cavalry and Light Dragoons "shall in future be carried on a waist-belt and not on a shoulder-belt as formerly".[2] It is worthy of note, however, that waist-belts "sufficient to carry a sword" were ordered in the Regulations for clothing of Dragoons as early as 1729.

The only scabbards of the eighteenth century that survive have frog-hooks, which show that they must have been worn in frogs, presumably longer than those worn by the Infantry. Thus it must have been a rather lengthy affair to take the swords from the frog and fix them to the saddle when dismounted as noted on p. 49.

The Infantry officer's sword was carried in the frog till 1822. With the *New Regulations* of that date the officer's scabbard was fitted with rings and the belt with slings was introduced; very attractive for ceremonial purposes but so inconvenient for the foot soldier or the dismounted cavalryman that a belt-hook was provided to hook up the sword when marching. These slings and hooks still survive in full dress and on sergeants' sword-belts.

In the first years of the nineteenth century, when even the fighting dress of the Cavalry was more suitable for the theatre than for active service, a new terror was introduced called the "sabretache"; as its name denotes, a pocket attached to the Cavalry sabre (Fig. 48).

Fig. 48.
Sabretache, 1814–1901.

This is fitted on the inside with a flap pocket, presumably to carry dispatches, the outside being emblazoned with the regimental badge or the Royal monogram as the case may be. It was

[1] W.O. 3/29, p. 130.   [2] W.O. 3/29, p. 40.

attached to the sword-belt with slings and those who have seen it in use will remember the wild flurry of sword and sabretache in full gallop. The sabretache is shown as worn by all ranks of Cavalry, including Household troops, in Hamilton-Smith's work which illustrates the *Dress Regulations* of 1814, and is ordered in all the *Dress Regulations* up to the year 1894. It was abolished in November 1901.[1]

THE "SAM BROWNE" BELT

The most important change in the sword-belt is the equipment universally known as the "Sam Browne" belt. In days gone by there has been a good deal of controversy as to the "true and onlie begetter" of this belt which has been copied by every army in the world. Its genesis arose when the officer had to carry revolver and sword, an impossible combination of various weights, on one waist-belt. The two versions of the story are as follows, and the reader is at liberty to make his own deductions.

In 1878 Sir Basil Montgomery of the 60th Rifles, who served in the Afghan campaign, had his belt made with braces by Indian saddlers and this belt from recent correspondence[2] seems to have been worn by General Sir Sam Browne. In the following year Sir James Douglas, R.H.A., fitted braces to his white leather belt during the Zulu War of that year, and in 1885 improved upon the pattern for the Staff of Sir Douglas Stewart at Umballa, the work being carried out by collar-maker Wittenden, R.H.A. Brown belts appear in the *Dress Regulations* of 1894, but the "Sam Browne" was not adopted as an official part of equipment till 24 April 1900. So there the matter must be left, but it should be urged that it is by no means impossible, when considering the extra weight to be carried on the belt, that two officers should independently have devised the same contrivance.

[1] War Office, A.O. 232.
[2] *Journal of Army Historical Research*, XIII, 243.

SWORD-KNOTS

The original purpose of the sword-knot was to form a loop round the hand so that the swords-man could recover his weapon if it was struck from his hand. Under Service conditions the sword-knot always was and is still of stout buff leather, but in full dress it was an elaborate appendage of gold cord and tassels. The knot was, and is now, twisted over the handguard and is only unloosed to go over the hand when the sword is used in action

Fig. 49. Sword-knot, 1790–1803.

(Figs. 2, 49). The sword-knot still survives in the useless cord and tassel which decorate the modern umbrella. The following are the main changes that have taken place in this detail of equipment.

General Officers
    1822. Crimson and gold cord and gold tassel.
    1831–1934. Crimson and gold cord and gold acorn.

Horse Guards
    1822. Crimson and gold, G.R. on crimson velvet slider, bullion tassel.
           Undress, white leather.
    1831. Crimson and gold leather strap with gold bullion tassel.
    1872. Crimson leather with gold and crimson tassel.
    1911. Crimson leather strap embroidered gold and crimson tassel.

Life Guards
    1831. Crimson and gold, gold bullion tassel.
           Undress, white leather strap.

1st Life Guards
    1872–1934. White leather with crimson and gold tassel.

2nd Life Guards
 1872–1934. Crimson leather with crimson and gold tassel.

Heavy Cavalry
 1822. Crimson and gold, bullion tassel.
 1831–1934. White leather, gold acorn.

Light Dragoons
 1822. Crimson and gold, bullion tassel.
 1834. White leather strap, gold acorn.
 1883. Crimson and gold cord, gold acorn.

Lancers and Hussars
 1834–1934. Crimson and gold cord, gold acorn. (The 13/18
  and 14/20 Hussars have no crimson.)

Royal Artillery
 1857. Gold strap and acorn.
 1872. Gold cord and acorn.
 1911–34. Gold cord with runner and acorn.

Royal Engineers
 1857. Gold braid and acorn.
 1861. Gold cord and acorn.
 1874. For regimental duty Russian leather and gold acorn.
 1883–1911. Gold cord and acorn.

Foot Guards
 1796. Crimson and gold.
 1822. Crimson and gold, bullion tassel.
 1857. Gold cord and acorn.
 1874. Crimson and gold strap, gold acorn.
 1883–1934. Gold cord and acorn.
  Undress—buff leather, gold acorn.

Infantry
 1796. Crimson and gold.
 1822. Crimson and gold, bullion tassel.
 1883–1934. Gold and crimson strap, gold acorn.

Rifles
    1822. Black leather.
    1911–34. Black leather strap and acorn.

Commissariat
    1864–83. Crimson and gold, gold tassel.

Army Service Corps
    1894–1934. Gold and blue cord and acorn.

Medical
    1861. Crimson and gold strap, gold acorn.
    1883. Gold and black cord and acorn.
    1894. Gold and black strap and acorn.
    1900–34. Gold and cherry coloured lace, gold acorn.

Ordnance
    1881–94. Gold and red cord, gold acorn.
    1900–34. Scarlet and gold strap, gold acorn.

Pay
    1864. As Commissariat.
    1881–1934. Yellow and gold cord and acorn.

Control Department
    1871–4. Blue and gold cord, gold acorn.

Military Train
    1859–64. Gold cord and acorn.

Lance, Bayonet, and Staff Weapons

AND A NOTE ON TESTS

LANCE, BAYONET, AND STAFF WEAPONS

THE LANCE[1]

The lance, which had been the principal weapon of the mounted man from the Norman Conquest up to the beginning of the seventeenth century, was for some unknown reason discarded for over 200 years, and till the end of the eighteenth century, with the exception of Oriental Light Cavalry, lances were not used in any of the European armies. It was to Napoleon that the general introduction of the lance into Europe was due, and the success of his "Polish" lancers convinced military authorities in England that the lance was a formidable weapon capable of producing a great moral effect on Infantry. On 21 September 1800–1, the 3rd French Hussars paraded with the lance, but the men were badly trained and according to Masson: "Ils ne tenaient pas une arme, ils portaient un gaule" (pole).[2] In 1816 experiments were conducted by Lord Rosslyn and Captain J. G. Peters,[3] of the 9th Light Dragoons, who trained men with 16-ft. lances bearing small union flags, and, on 29 April, a parade of fifty men of the 9th, 12th, 16th and 23rd Light Dragoons was held at Pimlico, the general public being admitted to inspect this new branch of the British Cavalry. Although the regiments were complimented by the King, there seems to have been severe criticism of their performance, for Colonel de Montmorency speaks of "the imperfections of the lance exercise by the three Pimlico Divisions so universally found fault with".[4] These remarks, taken in conjunction with Masson's account of the first French Lancers, go far to show that the lance is only a practical weapon after long and severe

[1] Reprinted from the *Army Quarterly*, xvii, by permission of the editor.
[2] F. Masson, *Cavaliers de Napoléon*, 1896.
[3] *Histories of the 9th and 16th Lancers.*
[4] Lieut.-Col. de Montmorency, *Exercises and Manœuvres of the Lance*, 1820.

training, an essential which is always insisted upon by all writers on the subject. The inordinate length of the staff—identically the same as that of Cromwell's infantry pikeman—was soon found to be impracticable, and a staff 9 ft. long was adopted early in the nineteenth century and, with variations of a few inches, has been the standard length ever since. Major A. S. Jones, V.C., writing in 1862, recommended an 11-ft. lance in order to make it superior to rifle and bayonet.

In 1881 Colonel Brix,[1] of the German General Staff, advocated a short lance of 6 ft., held near the butt, as a more convenient weapon, his views are also held by some authorities to-day, who have suggested that the "pig-sticking" spear is a better weapon than the 9-ft. service lance.

A variety of blades, including the small pike-point, the wide spear-head, and the leaf-shaped blade, were all tried, and eventually in 1860 the three-sided point, similar to that of the bayonet, was adopted.[2] In 1820 a steel ball about 2 in. in diameter was added to the base of the point to prevent undue penetration and to make withdrawal easier, which necessitated a heavier shoe to maintain the proper balance. In this year a wooden ball was carried on the point to guard against accidents in peace time, but it could not have been in use for long or in large numbers, as only two of these specimens are known to exist at the present day (Fig. 50).

In 1827 a committee was formed to decide upon a new pattern lance with Major-General Sir Hussey Vivian in the chair and Major Vandeleur of the Royal (12th) Lancers as one of the members. The lance under consideration was one of French pattern which General Mercer had brought back from Waterloo in 1815 and had deposited in the newly formed Rotunda Museum at Woolwich, whence it had been "abstracted" by Major Vandeleur, much to the annoyance of General Mercer.[3] The where-

---

[1] Lieut.-Col. Brix, *Gendanken über die Organisation u.s.w. der Cavalrie*, 1881.
[2] *List of Changes*, 180.
[3] *Journal of the Waterloo Campaign*, 1927.

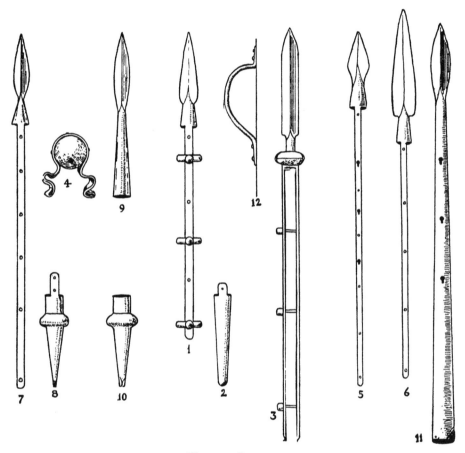

Fig. 50. Lances.

1. Head, 1816.
2. Shoe, 1816.
3. Head, 1820.
4. Point protector, 1820.
5. Head, 1840.
6. Head, 1846.
7. Head, 1860.
8. Shoe, 1860.
9. Head, 1868.
10. Shoe, 1868.
11. Experimental head, ? 1895.
12. Handguard.

abouts of this interesting weapon are at present unknown but it is believed to have been in the possession of Dr Hall in recent years. The committee sat from 23 April to 22 June and its recommendations received the Royal Approval on 24 February 1829. In the scanty records of its deliberations a drawing of Major Vandeleur's proposed lance is included, probably the earliest official pictorial record of any British Service weapon.[1]

At first using the Cromwellian pike as a model, the head was held by "langets" or "lanquets", that is, cheeks of steel, of varying lengths riveted to the staff, which were considered to be some protection against sword-cuts. In 1868 these were discarded and the head was socketed and fixed to the staff with shellac,[2] an innovation which was strongly criticized by many Cavalry officers, who instanced cases of lance-heads being cut off by Indian swordsmen.

Several suggestions were made to obviate this, Colonel G. Money, of the Central India Horse, producing a model of a lance-head with one langet to which the pennon was attached, and certain experimental lances were issued with socket-heads 22 in. long held in place with shellac and pins.

The langets were reintroduced in 1899.[3]

From 1816 to 1868 the staff was of ash impregnated with linseed oil and tar, but in 1836 the male bamboo was adopted.[4] The drawbacks of the bamboo were twofold, for the supply was never constant, and furthermore the Indian contractors frequently concealed worm holes and flaws by stoppings, so that it became almost essential to test every lance. Eventually, in 1885, the ash staff was reintroduced and was used when bamboo was not available. European armies experienced the same difficulties though they all favoured the bamboo for a staff (Fig. 51). France had great hopes from her colonies in Tonquin, but Germany, having no tropical colonies, experimented in 1890 with a steel staff, which is now the standard weapon and has

---

[1] War Office "Submissions", 1829.   [2] *List of Changes*, 180.
[3] *Ibid.* 5730.   [4] W.O. 3/281, p. 188.

been adopted also in the French Army. One of these experimental lances was made to unscrew in the centre, and a German trial lance was made to fold.

The pennon, after the first experiments with union flags, has always been a parti-coloured red and white flag attached in various ways: first, with brass eyelets fitting over three studs on bands at the lance-head and kept taut by a rubber strip, the studs being pierced to receive a thin locking rod; and later, by sewing the flag to a thin plate with studs which engaged in keyed slots in the langets.[1] From 1868 onwards the pennon was attached by hide laces passed through three eyelet holes. About the year 1840, a flimsy handguard of steel rod was tried, fastened to the staff over the grip with screws; but this, need-less to say, was very soon discarded, for even in peace time it was very easily knocked out of place (Fig. 50). The sling appears in all early patterns, but no records of the date of its use are found till 1884.

In 1883 a leather protector was added, both to provide a grip and to prevent the chafing of the staff by the carbine butt when slung.[2] In 1889, when the ash staff was reintroduced, the protector was dis-carded and a grip of white hide wrapped eight times round the staff at the balance point was substituted.[3] In 1896 a small

[1] Drouville, writing in 1813, suggested "shrill bells" hung underneath the union flag.
[2] *List of Changes*, 4451.   [3] *Ibid.* 5730.

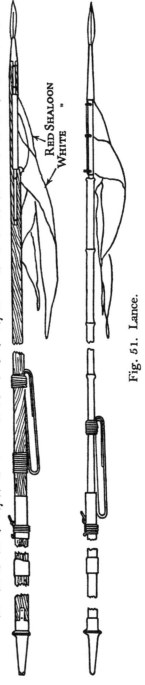

RED SHALOON
WHITE "

Fig. 51. Lance.

"D" ring was whipped to the staff, at first with a leather lacing and afterwards with wire, so that the lance resting in the lance bucket on the stirrup could be attached to the saddle when the rider dismounted.[1] This was evidently found to be inconvenient when remounting and was discontinued early in the present century.

The shoe at first had a blunt point socketed on to the butt. In 1860 this was superseded by a flanged shoe with square point and short langet, and in 1868 the langets were abolished and the shoe fixed like the head with shellac.

All through the nineteenth century military writers discussed the lance and its value, and, in view of the strong opinions expressed in its favour, it is interesting to find officers who had, in those days, reputations on Cavalry matters, writing in opposition.

Denison, who was the first modern writer to treat Cavalry operations exhaustively, considered that only half of the Heavy Cavalry should be armed with lances, the remainder with sabre and revolver; but he qualified this by saying that the lance can only be of use in the hands of a perfectly trained man and in a mêlée it is awkward and dangerous.[2] General Stephen Lee, quoted by Denison, strongly advocates the revolver as the favoured arm, but considers that if lancers exist they must also have swords, presumably for the same reasons put forward by Denison. Major-General Sir Charles MacGregor is definitely anti-lance, and states that he would not recommend the adoption of the lance in any Cavalry regiment except for highly trained men in Indian campaigns.[3]

Marmont[4] considered that it was essential for the second rank of Lancers to follow up with the sabre and Captain Nolan bears out Marmont's contention, for he describes a charge of the 16th Lancers at Aliwal in 1846, when many of the lancers were killed in the mêlée by Sikh infantry.[5] Major-General M. von Czerlieu

---

[1] *List of Changes*, 8366. [2] *Modern Cavalry*, 1868.
[3] *Life and Opinions of Major-General Sir C. MacGregor*, 1888.
[4] *Modern Armies*, 1888. [5] Captain Nolan, *Cavalry*, 1854.

of the Austrian Army, writing in 1901, is strongly against the lance for several reasons. First, because it is too "humane" and lance wounds are quickly healed; secondly, because it is more liable to break than the sword; and thirdly, because he considers that the "reach" of the swordsman is greater than that of the lancer. He further urges that it hinders rapid mounting and dismounting, it increases the weight carried by the horse, it is liable to betray the position of troops, tangles in woods and forests, and, in fact, has all the drawbacks and no advantages. He concludes by saying that the friends of the lance "are pursuing a phantom".[1]

On the other side, it is unnecessary to quote the views of all the advocates of the lance, for with the above exceptions all Cavalry officers and writers, of all nationalities, have expressed themselves strongly in its favour till the Boer War brought the rifle into prominence as a Cavalry weapon, and the War of 1914–18 produced an entire change in Cavalry operations.

In 1903 the lance was abolished except for ceremonial parades, and officers were reminded that in future the rifle was the chief weapon of the Cavalry.[2] In 1909, however, this order was rescinded and the lance again became the Service weapon of the Lancers,[3] only to be abolished again in 1927.[4]

The 16th Lancers claim to have been the first British regiment to use the lance in action in India about the year 1822, and from that date the Lancer regiments of the British Army have covered themselves with glory whenever they have been engaged.

In the late War the 12th Lancers were in action at Moy, on 28 August 1914, and the 9th Lancers on the Marne in September, while the Indian Lancers gave a good account of themselves in Palestine.

[1] *Journal of the Royal United Service Institution*, XLVII.
[2] A.O. 39, March 1903.
[3] A.O. 158, June 1909.
[4] A.O. 392, December 1927.

THE BAYONET

Most writers on the subject from the end of the seventeenth century have connected the name with the town of Bayonne, which certainly had a reputation for the manufacture of cutlery and crossbows, and they quote Menage's *Dictionary* published in 1694 and Voltaire's *Henriade* of a century later as authorities suggesting that the first bayonet was adapted from the crossbowman's knife made at Bayonne. Maréchal de Puységur[1] describes it as being 12 in. long. It had a crossguard and a wooden grip which fitted into the muzzle, the grip being tapered as none of the muskets of the period were standardized, and the calibres varied considerably. It had serious drawbacks: firstly, it could only be used after the musket had been discharged, which was at once proclaimed to the enemy by the fixing of bayonets; secondly, if rammed home, it was often difficult to unfix; and thirdly, if it were not securely fixed, it might be dropped or left in the body of the enemy (Plate III, 38; fig. 52).

Fig. 52.
Plug-Bayonet,
1680–1700.

The earliest mention of a bayonet used in the British Army is to be found in an account of operations in Tangiers in 1663, given in Sloan MSS. (British Museum) 1957, and ten years later a Warrant of Charles II, dated 2nd April 1672,[2] orders that Dragoons are to be provided with matchlocks and "one bayonet or great knife". The plug-bayonet continued in use till the beginning of the eighteenth century, when large numbers were returned to the Tower, where over 2000 bearing the Solingen mark were destroyed in the fire of 1841. Several specimens, however, still survive in the guard-room at Hampton Court.

The drawback of placing the musket out of action by fixing

---

[1] *Memoires*, chap. VIII, edit. 1747.   [2] W.O. 55/333, p. 148.

the bayonet was only realized after it had been in use for over a decade, and is credited to the French. Maréchal de Puységur describes a regiment shortly before the Peace of Nimeguen (1678) as having swords with rings at the grip which could be passed over the barrel and thus the piece could be fired with fixed bayonet.

By Warrant of 15 November 1678 Philip Russell was paid £8. 8s. for "a new sort of bayonet" but no details are given. It can hardly have been a plug-bayonet for this had been in use

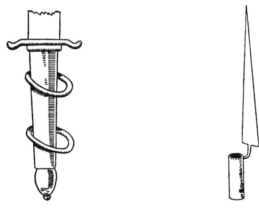

Fig. 53. Ring-Bayonet, 1689–1702.

Fig. 54. Socket-Bayonet, 1700.

for some years. It is possible that this was some form of socket-bayonet but, as will be seen below it is more probably the ringed variety. Mackay[1] attributes the invention of the ring-bayonet to a Highland officer in 1689, but it is more probable that, owing to the constant intercourse between Scotland and France at this period, the Highlander brought over the new-pattern weapon.

The illustration on Fig. 53 is taken from an engraving in Grose's *Military Antiquities* which was drawn by the Rev. Gostling who had seen Queen Anne's Life Guards armed with ring-bayonets. These loose-fitting rings had obvious disadvantages, and about the year 1703–4 the French introduced the

[1] *Memoirs of the Scottish War*, p. 52, edit. 1833.

socket-bayonet, fixed by a right-angled slot in the socket which passed over the sight and locked with half a turn (Fig. 54). This was by no means satisfactory, yet as late as 1843, according to Sir Sibald Scott,[1] the men of the 22nd Regiment at the battle of Meanee, in the Scinde Campaign, had their bayonets pulled off by the Bellochee enemy and had to tie them on with string and wire. In 1844 "A new and more secure method...for attaching or fixing the Bayonet" was introduced with springs to keep it in place and orders were issued for fitting these to existing bayonets.[2] From the year 1825 onwards experiments had been made with locking springs of different types, and eventually in 1853 a locking ring was fitted for the Enfield rifle. The blade was originally flat and dagger-like (Fig. 54). In 1745–6 the store vouchers record 15,000 bayonet scabbards as received in the Tower, but no mention is made of bayonets in this year.[3] Towards the end of the eighteenth century a triangular sectioned blade was introduced, the sides at first flat, though later, about 1825, they were "fullered" or grooved. The three-sided weapon was in use up to the year 1895, at first straight and in 1853 with a slight outward bend and latterly straight again (Figs. 55, A, B). Alongside this type was developed the true sword-bayonet first used with the Baker and Brunswick rifles in 1800 and 1837 respectively (Figs. 56–58). These were fixed on to side-brackets with locking springs in the brass grip. From 1853 onwards we have sword-bayonets for the Snider and Lancaster rifles with a ring in the quillon to fit over the barrel in addition to the grip-spring (Fig. 55, C, D). These weapons, although useful to some extent as swords, were destructive of balance of the rifle when used as bayonets, and the economical attempt to make one arm serve two purposes culminated in the preposterous Naval cutlass-bayonet, referred to on p. 87 (Fig. 60). An engraving by James Green, dated 1803, shows a cutlass-

---

[1] *Journal of the Royal United Service Institution*, VII.
[2] War Office Circular Memorandum 26 October 1844.
[3] W.O. 49/238.

bayonet as the arm of the Dismounted Light Horse Volunteers. An example of this type of weapon is preserved in the Tower (Fig. 59). Another and still more unpractical combination

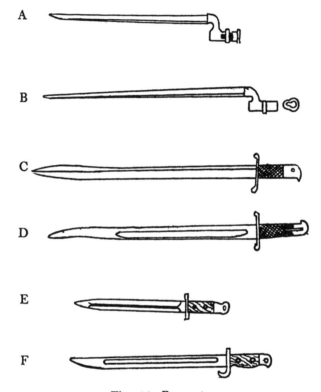

Fig. 55. Bayonets.

A. Martini-Henry, 1871.   D. Artillery, Mark III, ? 1870.
B. Martini-Enfield, 1883.   E. Pattern, 1888.
C. Lancaster, 1855.   F. Lee-Metford, 1907.

weapon was tried in the saw-back sword-bayonet, the set of the teeth preventing extreme penetration. In 1871 a broad leaf-shaped blade with saw-back, known as the "Elcho" was introduced which seems to have had a short life but was revived with certain alterations for the Ashanti campaign of 1895[1] (Fig. 61).

[1] Weedon Catalogue, 1899.

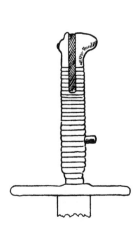

Fig. 56. Sword-Bayonet,
1st Baker Rifle, 1800.

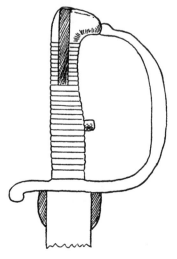

Fig. 57. Sword-Bayonet,
2nd Baker Rifle, 1801.

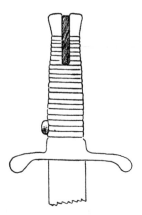

Fig. 58. Sword-Bayonet,
Brunswick Rifle, 1836.

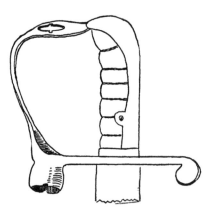

Fig. 59. Sword-Bayonet,
Light Cavalry, 1804.

This was followed in 1875 by the straight saw-backed sword-bayonet with knuckle-bow which was adopted by the Artillery

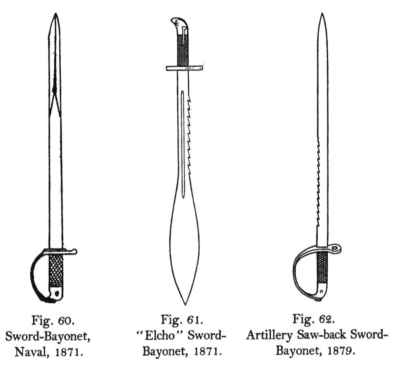

Fig. 60.
Sword-Bayonet,
Naval, 1871.

Fig. 61.
"Elcho" Sword-
Bayonet, 1871.

Fig. 62.
Artillery Saw-back Sword-
Bayonet, 1879.

(Fig. 62). In 1888 the short sword-bayonet was introduced and with variation of length and fitting has continued in use up to the present day, though it is within the bounds of possibility that this will experience drastic alterations before long.

STAFF WEAPONS

The names given to Staff weapons in different languages are often confusing in the extreme and it is difficult, without accompanying illustrations, to decide what type of weapon is referred to. The long pike, often as much as 15 ft. long, was the weapon of the Cromwellian Infantry, one of its uses being the protection it offered to Musketeers during the lengthy process of reloading. It was replaced by the matchlock and in 1702 flintlock musket and bayonet.[1] We are, however, concerned in these pages principally with the weapons carried by officers and sergeants in the late seventeenth and eighteenth centuries, and these were generally of similar type in England and in France. During the period when the matchlock was in use the Infantry sergeant, and for a longer period the Artillery sergeant, carried the lintstock, a combination of partizan blade and twin clips to hold slow match at which the musketeer and gunner could relight their matches (Fig. 63).

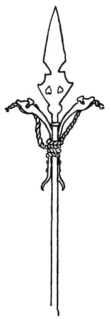

In the Royal Warrants halberds, pikes and espontoons are often mentioned. Warrant of 2 April 1672 twelve halberds are ordered for each troop of Dragoons and on 9 April 1677–8 the 2nd Dragoons had two partizans and six halberds, the former being carried by lieutenants.[2] In 1684 another Warrant orders the officers partizan to be exchanged for a pike. The partizan had a broad spear-point while the

Fig. 63. Lintstock, eighteenth century.

pike, or half-pike, as distinct from the 15-ft. pike of the Commonwealth, had a smaller point.

Maréchal de Puyésgur states that in 1703 the officers carried "espontons" 8 ft. long, and it may be that this is the weapon known in this country as the "spontoon".[3] In England, however, in the Duke of Cumberland's Regulations of 1743,[4] it is ordered that all officers of the Foot Guards are to carry spontoons in place of half-pikes. The half-pike, as the term implies,

---

[1] W.O. 26/11, p. 187.
[2] W.O. 55/333, p. 148 and W.O. 26/1, p. 267.
[3] *Art de la Guerre*, I, VI, 118.
[4] Captain T. Simes, *Military Guide*.

was the short, small-pointed survival of the Cromwellian long-pike, while the spontoon as we know it was a hybrid weapon, neither pike, partizan nor halberd, of only decorative value and of no use as a fighting weapon (Fig. 64).

An order dated 26 April 1769 runs: "If a General officer is at the head of his regiment (if Infantry) he takes post on foot, and of course, with his espontoon, doing every duty as Colonel. If

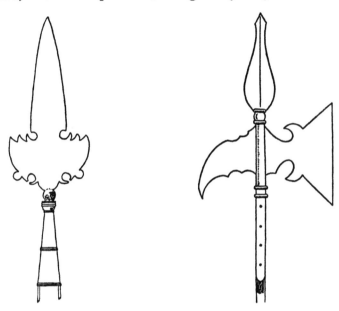

Fig. 64.
Officer's Spontoon, 1700–70.

Fig. 65.
Sergeant's Halberd, 1700–99.

it is a regiment of Dragoons he also takes post as Colonel and, when the regiment dismounts, he has his sword in his hand."[1]

On 17 April 1786 the spontoon was abolished and the officer carried a straight sword, the hilt silver or gilt according to the buttons of the regiment.[2]

The sergeant of the eighteenth century was armed with the halberd (Fig. 65), a most unpractical weapon when we consider the close formation of troops at this period. Three hundred years

[1] W.O. 3/24, p. 108.   [2] H.O. 50/380.

before the Swiss had realized this and substituted the pike as a more serviceable weapon. Grose[1] gives illustrations of the halberd exercise, but gives no explanation in the text. A return given on p. 43 states that in 1689 the Dragoons had no bayonets or halberds, but up to the present time we have been unable to discover any record, illustrated, printed or written, which might show how the 8-ft. halberd was carried by the Cavalry. These weapons can have been of little use except for "dressing" the ranks of Infantry, and for forming a triangle to which the prisoner was tied for flogging. In 1769 the sergeants of Grenadiers were ordered to have fusils, that is, short muskets instead of halberds,[2] but as will be seen below, the halberd was still carried by the Line regiments for twenty years.

In 1791 the following order was promulgated: "The Halberd now carried by sergeants of the infantry being confessedly a heavy unwieldy weapon, it has been represented to His Majesty that a pike or spear would be more convenient for carriage and more useful in the ranks."[3]

Trials were ordered of the comparative merits of the two weapons, and these were carried out by the 42nd and other regiments in October of the same year. Eventually, in February 1792, it was ordered that "the Halberd will gradually be laid aside and pikes, a new species of arms, substituted".

This change must have taken some time to carry out, for the coloured prints by Edward Dayes in the British Museum dated 1792 show sergeants of Foot Guards and Line regiments still carrying the halberd. The last halberd known to have been carried was that of the Drum-Major of the Oxford University Volunteers, who wielded this weapon with fine effect at the head of his band up to about the year 1880.[4]

The "new species of weapon" presents an interesting problem for the military antiquary in that Hogarth's "March to

[1] *Military Antiquities*, 1801.   [2] W.O. 3/24, p. 104.
[3] W.O. 3/10, pp. 72, 78, 96, 128.
[4] *Arms and Armour in the University of Oxford.*

Finchley", dated 1750, shows a pike with crossbar and also the halberd (Fig. 66). It is impossible to say if the pike is carried by an officer as the figure is lost in the crowd, but from this representation it is clear that the pike introduced in 1792 was by no means a new weapon. The next dated illustration of this pike, or the sergeant's "spontoon" as it was afterwards called, is to be found on a crude coloured print of regimental facings in the

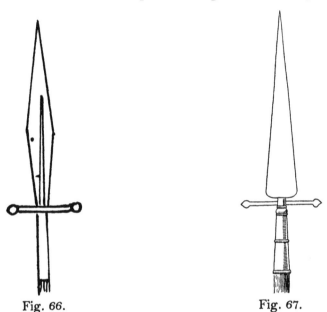

Fig. 66.
Sergeant's Pike, 1750.

Fig. 67.
Sergeant's Spontoon, 1800-30.

British Museum, dated 1803, whereon the same type of weapon with a different blade is shown. A number of these spontoons are exhibited in the Tower Armouries, many of which bear regimental numbers (Fig. 67).

The spontoon was abolished for Infantry in 1830[1] and according to tradition for Artillery in 1845.[2] A lithograph by Hull and Englemann dated 1830 shows the sergeant armed with the pike guarding the Ensign.

[1] War Office General Order, 31 July 1830, No. 491.
[2] No official order is recorded.

The Naval boarding pike is the true pike, but its shaft is stouter than that of the land weapon due to the rougher usage expected of it at sea. It ranks even before the sword as a direct descendant of the sapling used by primeval man, and for close-quarters, when associated with the cutlass, is a formidable weapon. It is impossible to date the introduction of the boarding pike, for it has always been used as spear or javelin whenever men at arms formed part of the ship's company throughout the ages. During the eighteenth and nineteenth centuries the Board of Ordnance supplied all weapons for the Navy, and it is more than probable that many of these were designed by soldiers without consulting the Navy. The Naval pike is a good example of this, for the early issues were made with a pointed iron shoe at the base which when "grounded" or "ordered" pierced the deck. The offending pikes were returned to the Ordnance and a ferrule substituted with open end through which the staff projected (Fig. 68). To those imbued with vivid imagination the scene may be conjured up of a naval commander

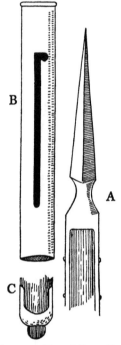

Fig. 68. Naval Boarding Pike, *circa* 1850–1926.

A. Point.
B. Protector.
C. Butt.

inspecting his decks after pike drill and the resulting communication sent through his admiral to the Admiralty and by them to the Board of Ordnance, and the hasty return of the ship to dockyard for the fitting of new deck planking.

An experimental point-protector was made about the year 1861 but never issued.

The only contemporary illustration of the Naval pike in action is to be found in the frontispiece of Brightman's *Life of Sir Philip Broke*. Boarding pikes are noted in the *Manual of Gunnery*,

1873, under "Sword bayonet and Pike exercise", but no details of the drill are given. They still appear as stores in the *Notes on Naval Guns*, 1893, corrected in 1899, and are listed as 15 for every 100 men. They were discontinued about the year 1900 and in June 1926, 1654 were returned to store[1] of which about 300 were distributed to Naval messes for decoration and to museums, the remainder being sold to officers and other accredited persons at 1s. 6d. each.

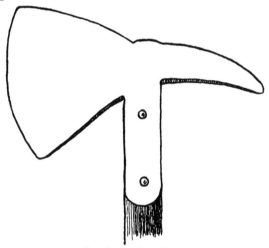

Fig. 69. Tomahawk or Boarding Axe, 1872–97.

The tomahawk is just a utility weapon with axe and pick head, a larger variety being the pole-axe carried by Farriers in the Household Cavalry to-day. By Royal Warrant of 21 February 1686–7 the Company of Miners, precursors of the Royal Engineers, were ordered "Extraordinary hammer-hatchets", the same weapon or tool being ordered for Dragoons. Three large pole-axes were ordered for the corporals of each company of the 1st Foot Guards by Royal Warrant of 28 June 1683 and a company of Grenadiers one hundred strong were equipped by Royal Warrant of 13 April 1678 with "103 hatchets with girdles". The tomahawk was the favoured weapon of the North American Indian as the British troops in America soon

[1] Admiralty Fleet Order 1534, 1926.

discovered to their cost. With a view to meeting like with like, the Ordnance issued 300 "Tommihawks" on 12 August 1761, to the 2nd Battalion of the Royal Americans.[1]

Tomahawks were officially issued with leather cases to the Royal Engineers in 1872[2] and were declared obsolete in 1897[3] (Fig. 69). There is no record of their issue to the Navy, but in 1926 there were still 163 in existence.

The Pioneer of the early nineteenth century carried the great "felling" axe (Fig. 70) which, it is somewhat surprising to find, was carried half a century earlier by Light Cavalry. A list of equipment of the Light Dragoons in 1756 gives, in addition to carbine, sword and pistols, spade, felling axe or hedging bill.[4] In 1838 the King's Dragoon Guards were issued "Hatchets with hammer-head" instead of "the Billhook used in the Peninsular". The order naïvely explains that "it may be considered to combine the properties of the hammer with those of the hatchet".[5]

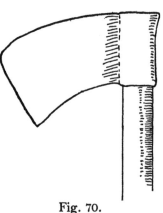

Fig. 70.
Pioneer's Felling Axe, 1815.

It should be noted that the "Battle Axe Company" of the Royal Artillery (No. 11 Western Battery) was so called merely because they won this weapon as a trophy at Martinique in 1809. Up to 1895, if not later, this axe was carried in front of the company by the tallest gunner who was allowed to wear moustaches.[6] The "Battle Axe Guard" mentioned in War Office Papers was merely a ceremonial guard similar to the Gentlemen-at-Arms. In 1803 this guard was formed by a company of Foot Guards on duty at Government House, Dublin.[7]

[1] W.O. 34/4, p. 156.   [2] *List of Changes*, 2306.   [3] *Ibid.* 8884.
[4] W.O. 30/13 A, p. 3.   [5] W.O. 3/132, p. 340.
[6] Chichester, H. M. and G. Burges-Short, *Records and Badges of the British Army*.   [7] H.O. 51/150, p. 257.

TESTS

In the compass of the present work, which is intended to deal rather with the historical aspect of weapons than with its manufacture and technical details, it would be obviously out of place to go deeply into the composition of the metal and description of machinery employed in sword manufacture. As, however, mention is made of the difficulties experienced in testing during the 1885 controversy, it may be of interest to describe broadly the tests to which the principal weapons are subjected. The steel blank, about $17 \times 1\frac{1}{4} \times \frac{1}{2}$ in., is heated and drawn out under a machine hammer till it is about 36 in. long. It is then reheated and passed between rollers which form the "fullers" or grooves. The "tang", or portion of the sword which passes through the grip, is then formed and the blade roughly shaped. It is hardened, in oil cooled with water, till it becomes quite brittle and is tempered in molten lead. The adjustments for straightness or curve, as the case may be, are made by hand, for no machine has been devised which can take the place of the human eye and the intuition of the skilled craftsman, a condition which has persisted since the first sword was made in the Bronze Age three thousand years ago. The next operation is the grinding of the blade, and the softening of the tang. The blade, and afterwards the complete sword, is subjected to the following tests, and finally, in the case of officers' swords, it is polished and "embossed". This consists of painting by hand or transfer those portions which are to remain bright, the remaining being etched with dilute nitric acid. The gilding, if any, is done by mercuria deposit and the "blueing" by the application of heat.

SWORD TESTS

The blade is tested by hand, striking its back, edge and both flats on an oak block. The hilt and blade are assembled and a moderate blow struck on back and edge to test soundness of hilting. In 1788 it was ordered that swords should be tested by being "struck by a strong hand on a hard board and bent in a special machine at the rate of 2 inches to 1 foot at least".[1] In 1796 they had to undergo "most accurate proof".[2]

The blade is also subjected to vertical tests in a machine. The figures in column A give the number of pounds weight applied, after which the blade, still under the weight, must recover straightness after depression of 1 in. Column B is the same test with hilt and blade assembled. Column C gives the number of inches of depression in the same machine but without the weight. The blade is depressed to right and to left, and must recover straightness after each depression.

	A lb.	B lb.	C in.
Cavalry	32	30	5
Royal Artillery and Royal Army Service	26	24	4½
Infantry, Ordnance, Pay, etc.	32	30	4
Highland Regiments ("claymore")	18	16	5
Rifle Regiments	17	15	4
Royal Army Medical	20	18	4

Where the decoration of handguards of swords includes piercing of the guard, it is laid down from 1895 onwards that the piercing must not be sufficiently large to admit the point of sword, lance or bayonet.

BAYONET TESTS

The Martini-Henry Bayonet was tested by inserting the point in a socket and bending the bayonet over an arch of wood having an elevation of 2½ in. in the centre. The socket end must be bent over to the extent of 4 in. and the bayonet must spring back perfectly straight. The same test is applied to all three sides.[3]

The 1907 bayonet is subjected to the same striking test as the sword, but this is done by a machine and not by hand. In the

[1] W.O. 3/37, p. 36.   [2] W.O. 3/29, p. 44.
[3] A similar test was employed for swords in 1885 but was discarded later in favour of the vertical-pressure test.

vertical machine it is subjected to a weight of 110 lb. and must recover straightness after depression of about ¾ in. It is then sprung round a wood block similar to that used for the Martini-Henry bayonet and finally the several parts are gauged.

LANCE TESTS

The Lance is tested as follows: the point is fixed in a bench-clip and as the point is tapered this raises the socket above the level plate beneath the clip. A weight of 56 lb. is applied to the staff about 21 in. from the point so as to bring the under-surface of the whole of the point coinciding with the level plate. This is applied to all three sides of the point and in each case it must spring back straight when the weight is raised.

The assembled lance is sprung by compression to a deflection of 6 in. and must recover straightness.

APPENDIX

Muskets, Rifles, and Carbines

APPENDIX

MUSKETS, RIFLES, AND CARBINES

The whole history of firearms has been so fully dealt with in technical works that it would be unnecessary to recapitulate all the experimental work carried out during the nineteenth century in order to produce a satisfactory weapon for the Army. For this the bibliography at the end of this volume gives the titles of the most useful works on the subject. We will therefore confine ourselves to a bare recital of the several patterns in use at various periods with the reasons for their adoption.

The earliest form, the hand-gun, a tube of iron closed at one end and fired by a slow match, was in use during the fifteenth and sixteenth centuries at a period before the Army as an organization existed.

In the middle of the sixteenth century a contrivance appears by which the match, instead of being held in the hand, was fixed in a clip or "serpentine" which was lowered or raised by a trigger derived from the "tricker" of the crossbow. There were serious drawbacks to this weapon known as the "matchlock". Firstly, it was very heavy and necessitated the use of a forked rest to support the muzzle; secondly, it took so long to load, between thirty and forty operations, that the musketeer had to retire under the long pikes of the Infantry for safety;[1] thirdly, the lighted slow match proclaimed to the enemy the presence of musketeers and lastly there was always the danger of ammunition being exploded accidentally by these lighted matches. It is needless to point out that wet weather might put the whole army out of action.

The wheel-lock, a mechanical contrivance in which a serrated wheel actuated by a spring revolves against a piece of iron pyrites was so costly to produce that it was never used on a large scale. In spite of its complicated mechanism it was carried by the Cavalier or Cuirassier of the Commonwealth

[1] De Gheyn, *Exercise of Armes for Calivers, Muskettes and Pikes*, 1607.

(127)

period. Cruso, in his *Militarie Instructions for the Cavallrie*, 1632, describes it as a "firelock, the barrell of 18 inches long". About the year 1640 the "miquelet" or snaphaunce made its appearance in Spain and was adopted all over Europe. This consisted of a cock in which was held a piece of flint which on pulling the trigger struck a steel hammer and produced sparks which ignited "mealed" powder in the pan which communicated with the vent or touch-hole. Here again there were drawbacks, for the flint misfired and the powder in the pan often got wet or was blown away.

By Warrant of 14 April 1660[1] Monck ordered the Ordnance to replace matchlocks by snaphaunces, but in 1672[2] matchlock muskets were specifically ordered for the Dragoons raised for service in the Barbados. By another Warrant dated 21 February 1687 the regiments of Foot are ordered matchlocks and snaphaunces, but the Dragoons are particularly mentioned as carrying the snaphaunce.[3]

The Earl of Orrery,[4] in describing the efficiency of the flint-lock as compared with the matchlock, writes that "you have only to cock and you are prepared to shoot". He describes the difficulties of "blowing the match in hedge fights or sieges", and states that the match is "very dangerous where bandoliers are used or where soldiers have to run hastily to the budge-barrel to refill their bandoliers; I have often seen sad instances thereof". He concludes by pointing out that the lighted match will "inform the enemy where you are" and instances cases of a high wind blowing away the powder "ere the match can touch the pan". The match was an appreciable addition to the baggage carried. In 1742 there were 2 tons of match stored in the Tower and in the following year 14 tons are recorded.[5]

The flintlock, an improvement on the miquelet, was invented

---

[1] Colonel Clifford Walton, *The British Standing Army*, Appendix.
[2] See p. 43.   [3] Walton, *loc. cit.* p. 423.
[4] *Treatise on the Art of War*, 1677.
[5] W.O. 49/238. This was both for artillery and musketeers.

to obviate one of these difficulties. There is no satisfactory evidence as to which country was responsible for this improvement, Spain, France and Germany claiming the honours. Here the hammer and pan cover are combined in such a way that the powder is kept dry and when the piece is fired the hammer flies up and at the same instant uncovers the priming powder for the spark (Fig. 71). The flintlock came to be adopted by every military body all over the world and is still in use among some undeveloped Oriental nations. We have stated that one of the objections to this arm was that the flint and steel often missed fire and this was considered to be so serious that the matchlock

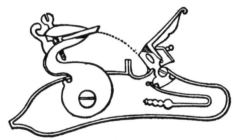

Fig. 71. Flintlock, 1790–1840.

persisted in the English Army till 1690, when it was abolished in favour of the flintlock, by Warrant of 14 April.

There were three sizes of flintlock in use in the middle of the eighteenth century; the musket, the fusil or "fuzee"—a short musket—and the carbine. The calibres ranged from ·70 to ·85, a variation which must have created serious difficulties in regard to supply of bullets and bayonets on active service.

Muskets were made by gunmakers in London, especially in the Minories near the Tower. There were local factories in Birmingham and in 1759 3,000 muskets are recorded as coming from Dublin. The supply was never sufficient to meet the demand, for in 1799 no less than 40,000 were imported from Liége and more from Hamburg.

This became such a serious matter that about the year 1804 the factory at Enfield was built and numbers of walnut trees were

planted for making gun-stocks. At first a semi-private under-
taking, the Enfield works were acquired by the Government in
1812, and here barrels were made, and locks, made at the Tower,
were assembled. Between the years 1855–9 the works were
considerably enlarged and at the end of this period the gun-
makers' contracts were closed as the factory could produce
130,000 muskets and bayonets a year.[1]

The Infantry carried the musket and bayonet with a "hanger"
as a "last resort", the sergeants and, in some regiments, the
officers having their halberds and spontoons replaced by fusils.[2]

The Cavalry seem to have carried both musket and carbine,
for in 1767 the Dragoons are noted as having firelocks, carbines
and bayonets. In 1796 a Report of the Board recommends that
the firelock or musket should be cut down to 26 in. till a new
carbine can be provided and that a swivel-bar be added. This
bar had a running ring upon it for attachment to the trooper's
cross-belt.[3] In addition the Cavalry had flintlock pistols of the
same bore as the musket weapons they had carried since 1689.[4]
In 1747 Dragoons marched past with musket and bayonet fixed.[5]
With the nineteenth century the musket was abolished for
Cavalry and the short flintlock carbine substituted without a
bayonet, the only known exception to this being the sword
bayonet of the Light Horse above alluded to. It would be
tedious to recapitulate the varieties of flintlock carbine which
include Baker, Elliott, Paget, Manton, most of which are of ·653
or ·730 calibre.

The calibres of the musket of the Infantry varied as did that of
the carbine, ranging from ·684 to ·758, the majority being ·753.
The typical musket of the period, known as "Brown Bess", was
of this calibre, the barrel being fixed to the stock by lugs under
the barrel held by sliding pins through the stock and not by

[1] Lord Cottisloe, *Journal of Army History Research*, XII, 197.
[2] T. 14/13, p. 392.   [3] W.O. 3/29, p. 42.   [4] S.P. 44/167.
[5] "On Sat. 31 Jan. the Duke of Cumberland marched past the King at the head
of his Regiment with musket and fixed bayonet." *Penny London Post*, 1747.

bands (Fig. 72). It has been recorded above that the figures of infantrymen at the base of the statue of the Duke of Wellington, erected to record the prowess of the British Army, are armed with French flintlock muskets and not with the "Brown Bess", a warning to sculptors to study historical detail. An example of the difficulties caused by non-standardization of weapons is the defeat of the King's German Legion at La Haye Sainte during the battle of Waterloo due to the fact that the ammunition served out to them did not fit their muskets.[1] In the middle of the eighteenth century, when Grenadiers were attached to each regiment, experimental grenade muskets were produced. One type had the grenade-cup screwed on to the muzzle, the grenade being expelled by the normal musket charge, and another far more dangerous had the cup at the butt with a separate charge. Both of these, however, were too complicated for general use.

Rifling had been known since the sixteenth century, but it was not employed in any army till the eighteenth century. In 1776 Colonel Ferguson brought out a breech-loading rifle which was used in small numbers by British troops in America, and in 1798 a rifle battalion was formed in the Royal American Regiment (60th). In the year 1800 the rifle was introduced into the British Army by Ezekiel Baker who produced his First and Second Rifles in 1800 and 1801. The difficulty of the muzzle-loading rifle was that the ball had to be of such dimensions as to run down the barrel and yet had to be spread at the breech end to fit the rifling, and ramming down tended to compress the powder. The methods for solving this problem will be described later on in this chapter.

We now come to an epoch-making invention which revolutionized the principle of gunnery all over the world. In 1806 a Scottish minister, the Rev. Alexander Forsyth, brought a gun to London in which the charge was ignited by a direct flash from a composition of detonating powder with no intervening pan.

[1] Wellington admitted his responsibility for this. Sir W. Fraser, *Words on Wellington*, p. 237.

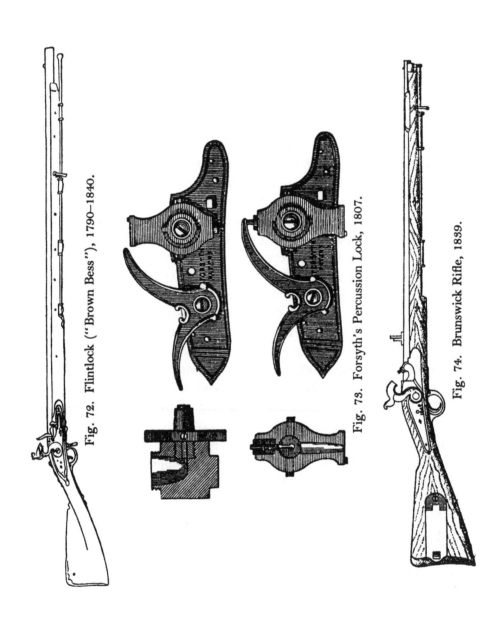

Fig. 72. Flintlock ("Brown Bess"), 1790–1840.

Fig. 73. Forsyth's Percussion Lock, 1807.

Fig. 74. Brunswick Rifle, 1839.

This so impressed Lord Moira, Master General of Ordnance, that he invited Forsyth to experiment for the Government in special workshops at the Tower, £100 being allotted to him for his work. The process of compounding the detonators was so dangerous that Forsyth could get no assistants and had to rely upon himself. With a change of Ministry in April 1807 Forsyth was turned out of the Tower "with all his rubbish" and retired to perfect his invention which he patented in 1807 (Fig. 73). There is a legend that Napoleon offered £20,000 for the percussion lock and that Wellington scoffed at it; but it should be remembered that Forsyth's lock was costly to make and that Wellington was engaged in long-drawn operations which could not be delayed by the introduction of a new weapon, however efficient it might be. In the course of time Forsyth's lock was adopted by sportsmen all over Europe and at long last, in 1834, the War Office made a trial at Woolwich of six flintlocks against six of the new percussion muskets with the result that out of 6000 rounds the percussion lock won with the proportion of one mis-fire against twenty-six of the flintlock. At first the detonating was effected by inserting small tubes or primers in place of Forsyth's somewhat elaborate magazines and in or about 1836 a copper cap by Westley-Richards was introduced, based on the previous invention of Captain Shaw of Philadelphia.

The new arm now became a practical proposition and the 3rd Grenadier and 1st Coldstream Guards made trials with such satisfactory results that in 1839 the 2nd Battalion of the Rifle Brigade were com-pletely armed with a percussion rifle known as the "Brunswick"[1] (Fig. 74). The peculiarities of this rifle was that the ball had a belt which fitted the grooves of the rifle (Fig. 75). In 1840–2 all the flintlock smooth-bore muskets were converted to percussion, the 2nd Border Regiment claiming the distinction of being the first to use the

Fig. 75. Brunswick Belted Ball, 1839.

[1] Hon. T. F. Fremantle, *The Book of the Rifle*, p. 31.

new arm in action at Amoy on 26 August 1841. After much undignified haggling the Government awarded Forsyth £1000, the first instalment being paid on the day of his death, 11 June 1843. A tablet was erected in the Tower to Forsyth's memory on 30 January 1930.

In 1840 the pistol was abolished as a Cavalry arm and the carbine and sword alone retained.[1]

The Cavalry and Artillery carbines followed the Infantry musket; Westley-Richards, Manton, Paget and Blanchard producing percussion arms all of different calibres and all of them

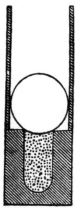 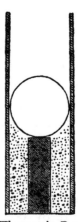

Fig. 76. Delvigne Breech, 1826.   Fig. 77. Thouvenin Breech, 1828.

smooth bore and eventually in 1834 serious notice was taken of this unsatisfactory condition.[2] With regard to this question of calibre, it is somewhat remarkable to find that a large bore was favoured for the musket of 1842 because the balls of the French, Belgian, Russian and Austrian armies could be fired out of our barrels whilst our balls could not be fired out of their arms.[3]

In the meanwhile all nations had been trying to overcome the difficulties of the muzzle-loading rifle. The chambered-breech of Delvigne and the pillar-breech of Colonel Thouvenin for expanding the bullet with other contrivances were all tested with

[1] W.O. 3/95, p. 57.   [2] W.O. 3/87.
[3] Lieut.-Col. H. Bond, *Treatise on Military Small Arms*, 1884, p. 196.

unsatisfactory results[1] (Figs. 76, 77). Eventually, Captain Minié, Instructor of the school at Vincennes, produced a bullet with a small iron cup set in a cavity at the base (Fig. 78). On the explosion of the charge the iron cup forced the sides of the bullet into the grooves, thereby stopping windage. Minié's bullet was used in 1851 with a new pattern rifle named erroneously the "Minié", for it was only the bullet that was Minié's invention, the rifle being produced at Enfield. This arm was used in the Kaffir War and in the Crimea. Minié is stated to have received £20,000 from the British Government for his invention, but after trial it was evident that something simpler was needed and in 1853 a bullet devised by Mr Metford was adopted with the Enfield rifle and was introduced into the Army in 1855 having replaced the Minié of 1851 and the smooth-bore musket of 1842.[2] For the next ten years the battle raged over the subject of rifling. Colonel Jacob of the Bombay Artillery at his own expense conducted a long series of experiments,[3] and at home Westley-Richards, Lancaster and Wilkinson all put forward suggested improvements. By this time the Enfield factory had taken over the manufacture of small arms which had hitherto been carried out by contracts with gun-makers. A committee

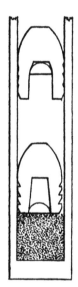

Fig. 78.
Minié Bullet,
1847.

was formed in 1854 which, after asking 7933 questions, deputed Mr (afterwards Sir Joseph) Whitworth to conduct experiments with a hexagonal bullet, his out-of-pocket expenses totalling £12,000.[4] In 1863 a pattern of the Whitworth rifle was ap-

---

[1] *Ibid.* p. 200; Graham, *History of the 16th Light Dragoons*, I, 143.

[2] Lieut.-Col. H. Bond states that this bullet was invented by Pritchett but this is an error as Pritchett afterwards acknowledged that the credit was due to Metford.   [3] H. Deane, *Manual of Firearms*, 1858, p. 263.

[4] H. Busk, *The Rifle*, 1858, p. 92.

proved and 8000 were ordered to be made at Enfield but were never issued. While the Infantry had to be content with a muzzle-loading arm the Cavalry were testing breech-loading carbines, for muzzle-loading on horseback is a difficult process. Sharp, Terry, Mountstorm, Green and Westley-Richards all submitted patterns, the Sharp carbine being, according to tradition, the origin of the term "Sharpshooters" used in the American Civil War. Terry's arm gave satisfactory results in 1858 when 1800 rounds were fired on board H.M.S. *Excellent* without cleaning. The details of all these are far too technical for description here and readers are referred to the standard works on firearms.[1]

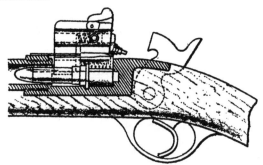

Fig. 79. Snider Breech, 1866–71.

By the year 1859 the Royal Small Arms Factory had been completed and the very unsatisfactory outside contracts with gun-makers came to an end. In 1860 all parts of the rifle were so carefully gauged as to be interchangeable, "an incalculable advantage for a military arm, particularly in the field". It was further laid down "that the Army shall be equipped exclusively with rifles of an interchangeable pattern".[2] The chief objective therefore of the War Department was to convert the Enfield rifle into a breech-loader and after fifty specimens had been submitted the Snider system was adopted in 1866 (Fig. 79). As was

[1] Hon. T. F. Fremantle, *The Book of the Rifle.* H. Ommundsen and E. H. Robinson, *Rifles and Ammunition.*
[2] *Text Book of Small Arms*, 1888, p. 107.

the case with a former inventor, Alexander Forsyth, Snider never lived to receive payment for his invention and died the same year. It is of some interest to note that in the Tower Armouries are two carbines of Henry VIII which have the Snider breech, an invention which was never improved upon and lay dormant till Snider reinvented it.

The Snider was first used by the King's Own Royal Regiment in 1868, and by this time all muzzle-loading rifles and carbines were converted. It was never perfect, as it was heavy and had an unsatisfactory extractor, the cartridge having to be "picked out by hand" or the rifle turned over

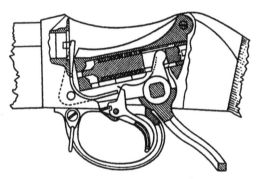

Fig. 80. Martini-Henry Breech, 1871.

sideways for it to drop out! This conversion was at best a makeshift and the year of its adoption, 1866, saw a new committee formed who inspected 120 arms and 49 descriptions of ammunition, but came to no decision. They renewed their investigations in 1867 and after examining a further 45 specimens decided on the Martini action with a Henry rifling (Fig. 80). Friedrich von Martini was an Austrian Engineer officer who, when he had perfected his breech-mechanism, set up an embroidery factory at Witte-am-Rhein. His invention is mainly based on the breech-loader of Peabody patented in 1865. Henry was an Edinburgh gunsmith and military enthusiast, so much so that he sat up all night so as to be the first volunteer enrolled in the Queen's Edinburgh Rifles in 1859, when the famous "Letter of the Four Colonels" to Napoleon III nearly precipitated a war between England and France.

Still the experiments went on; the Henry rifling being replaced by that of Metford and later on the Enfield rifling was tried. In 1883 it was considered essential to produce a magazine rifle to counter the efforts of France, Russia, Norway, Sweden, Italy and Turkey, who were all testing the Kropatschek, the Evans, the Schuloff, the Mannlicher, the Crag-Petersen, the Vetterli and the Winchester rifles. Germany was in advance of the rest of Europe and issued 2000 Mauser repeaters for test. Eventually the Lee-Metford was adopted in 1888, the rifling by Metford, a very distinguished civil engineer, and the magazine by Lee, a Scottish-Canadian watchmaker. In 1895 the Enfield rifling was adopted in place of the Metford and from this date various improvements and alterations have been made. The Cavalry and Artillery carbines which followed the patterns of the Infantry arms were abolished in 1902 in favour of the short Lee-Enfield of that date.

In all about 150 forms of firearms have been used in the British Army from the matchlock onwards. Many of the improvements and alterations have been very small, but each shows some small advance on the efficiency of its predecessor.

WORKS CONSULTED

Public Record Office: under sections A.O.; H.O.; T; W.O.

War Office: Circular Letters, Memoranda, Orders, rare military books, etc.

British Museum: various MSS.

Abridgement of the English Military Discipline, 1686.

ANGELO and ROWLANDSON. *The Hungarian and Highland Broadsword*, 1799.

Army Equipment, 1865–6.

Army Quarterly, vol. XVII.

BOND, Lieut.-Col. H. *Treatise on Military Small-Arms*, 1884.

BRACK, General A. F. DE. *Avant-postes de cavalérie légère*, 1834.

BRIX, Lieut.-Col. L. A. *Gedanken über die Organisation, u.s.w. der Cavalrie*, 1881.

BUSK, H. *The Rifle*, 1858.

Cavalry Journal, vols. I, II, VI.

CHICHESTER, H. M. and G. BURGES-SHORT. *Records and Badges of the British Army*, 1900.

CLEAVELAND. *Notes on the Early History of the Royal Regiment of Artillery*. N.d.

Command Paper 5633, 1889 (Cavalry Sword and Pistol at Suakim).

Costume of the Army of the British Empire. By an Officer on the Staff, 1814.

Costume of the British Army, 1828–30. Hull and Englemann.

Creevy Papers, edit. 1912.

DEANE, H. *Manual of Firearms*, 1858.

DENISON, Lieut.-Col. G. T. *Modern Cavalry*, 1868.

Dress Regulations, sub annis.

DROUVILLE, Captain J. *Formation of British Lancers*, 1813. (War Office Library.)

Exercise for Horse, Dragoons and Foot Forces, 1739.

FAUVERT-BASTONAL, *Lance et Sabre*, 1897. (War Office Library.)

FFOULKES, CHARLES. *Arms and Armour in the University of Oxford*, 1912.

—— *Inventory and Survey of the Armouries of the Tower of London*, 1916.

FREMANTLE, Hon. T. F. *The Book of the Rifle*, 1901.

GAYA, LOUIS DE. *Traité des Armes*, edit. 1911.

GHEYN, JACOB DE. *Exercise of Arms for Calivers, Muskets and Pikes*, 1607.

GRAHAM, Col. H. *History of the 16th Queen's Light Dragoons*, vol. I, 1912.

GROSE, F. *Military Antiquities*, edit. 1801.

HINDE, Captain R. *Discipline of the Light Horse*, 1778.

Histories of the 9th and 17th Lancers.

WORKS CONSULTED

Journal of Army Historical Research, passim.

Lance Exercise, Cutliffe, 1816–17. (War Office Library.)

List of Changes, sub annis.

MacGregor, Lady. *Life and opinions of Maj.-Gen. Sir C. MacGregor*, 1888.

Marey, Colonel. *Mémoire sur les Armes Blanches*, 1841.

Marmont, Marshal A. F. *Modern Armies*, trans. by Captain Lendy, 1865.

Masson, F. *Cavaliers de Napoléon*, 1896.

Mercer, General C. *Journal of the Waterloo Campaign*, 1870.

Montmorency, Lieut.-Col. R. H. de. *Rules and Regulations for the Exercise and Manœuvres of the Lance*, 1820.

Nolan, Captain L. E. *Cavalry*, 1853.

Ommundsen, H. and E. H. Robinson. *Rifles and Ammunition*, 1915.

Orrery, Earl of. *Treatise of the Art of War*, 1677.

Parliamentary Paper VI. XX. XXII.

Pelet-Narbonne, Lieut.-Gen. G. von. *La Service des Rapports, etc. de la Cavalérie*, 1887.

Proceedings of the House of Commons, 11 November 1690.

Puységur, Maréchal J.-F de. *Art de la Guerre*, 1749.

Report of the Committee on Swords, 0997, 1885.

Representation of Cloathing of His Majesty's Forces, 1742.

Royal United Services Institution Journal, vols. VI, VII, XXXIII, XLVII, XLIX.

Saxe, Marshal de. *Les Rêveries*, 1756.

Scott, Sir S. *The British Army*, 1867.

Simes, Captain T. *Military Guide for Young Officers*, 1781.

Text Book on Small Arms, 1884, 1888.

Walton, Colonel Clifford. *The British Standing Army*, 1894.

INDEX

INDEX

For EU product safety concerns, contact us at Calle de José Abascal, 56–1°,
28003 Madrid, Spain or eugpsr@cambridge.org.